That Rough Beast, Its Hour Come Round at Last:

The History of Hurricane Katrina

That Rough Beast, Its Hour Come Round at Last:

The History of Hurricane Katrina

Edited by
Heather Andrews, Tameika Ashford, Joshua Bowen,
Brandon Cooper, Lesley Cort, Michael Dunican,
Steven Rydarowski, Melanie Sweeney

Texas Review Press
Huntsville, Texas

FIRST EDITION, 2007

Requests for permission to reproduce material from this work should be sent to:

    Permissions
    Texas Review Press
    English Department
    Sam Houston State University
    Huntsville, TX 77341-2146

Library of Congress Cataloging-in-Publication Data

That rough beast, its hour come round at last : a history of Hurricane Katrina /
Heather Andrews ... [et al.]. -- 1st ed.
    p. cm.
 ISBN-13: 978-1-933896-00-7 (pbk. : alk. paper)
 ISBN-10: 1-933896-00-0 (pbk. : alk. paper)
 1. Hurricane Katrina, 2005--History. I. Andrews, Heather.
 QC945.T57 2007
 976'.044--dc22
                         2007014880

This book is dedicated to the residents of
Alabama, Louisiana, and Mississippi whose lives were so severely
impacted by the devastation of Hurricane Katrina.

Publisher's Note

This book was produced by my Editing/Publishing class at Sam Houston State University during the fall of 2006. Students did all the research and the writing and then designed the book from beginning to end, including the striking cover. They were also responsible for final editing. (If you find errors, blame them on the editors.)

The reason for choosing this particular subject for the class project was simply that the students could think of no more significant an event in recent years that deserved the attention that this storm and its devastation did.

There are, of course, many books on Katrina in circulation now—and there were several out when this project started—so why add to such a growing canon of publications on the storm? The class came up with two answers: the breadth of the book, which traces the storm from its inception through its dissolution inland, and the photographs, most of which have never been seen in print before.

I have served as a newspaper columnist for many years now, and over those years I have also done numerous feature stories, among them several pieces on the post-Katrina Mississippi Coast and Lower Ninth Ward of New Orleans. In the process of writing those stories, I took hundreds of photographs in the aftermath of the storm. Many of those never-seen-before photos appear in this collection.

A graduate student of mine, Michael Dunican, also spent a great deal of time on the Mississippi and Alabama Coasts and in the Lower Ninth Ward, and many of his original photographs appear in this book.

In addition to the photographs taken by me and Michael, we have incorporated a number of excerpts from interviews we conducted with survivors of the storm.

Hence, though much of this book is a repeat of information the reader may have read before, we promise exciting new dimensions.

—Paul Ruffin, Director, Texas Review Press

Table of Contents

That Rough Beast, Its Hour Come Round at Last:

The History of Hurricane Katrina

The Formation of Hurricane Katrina: The Beast That Was

Katrina was a potent hurricane that left a bitter taste in the mouths of many Americans who made their homes in southern Louisiana and along the Mississippi Gulf Coast. It was the most costly hurricane ever to strike the United States. Katrina first swept across Florida as a Category 1 on the Saffir-Simpson Hurricane Scale. After reaching Category 5 intensity over the central Gulf of Mexico, Katrina weakened to a Category 3 before making landfall. The damages and loss of life inflicted by this massive hurricane in Louisiana and Mississippi were staggering. The effects extended as far east as the Florida panhandle and as far north as Pennsylvania.

The complex genesis of the storm began as a tropical wave, a tropospheric trough, and the remnants of Tropical Depression Ten. This trough, located over the western Atlantic and the Bahamas, produced a strong wind shear across Tropical Depression Ten and caused it to degenerate on 14 August 2005 about 825 miles east of Barbados. The trough weakened as it moved westward toward Florida. The wind shear weakened enough to allow a new system to develop into a tropical depression by 1800 UTC*, 23 August, over the Bahamas, about 175 miles southeast of Nassau. The depression was designated Tropical Depression Twelve. An inner core formed and evolved into a deeper cyclone and became subject to a middle- to upper-tropospheric ridge over the northern Gulf and southern United States on 24 August. The ridge diverted the storm—assigned the name Katrina by the National Weather Service (NWS)—westward toward Florida. The storm continued to strengthen, and Katrina was estimated to have reached hurricane status near 2100, 25 August, less than two hours before making its first landfall in the United States near the Miami-Dade and Broward County line with maximum sustained winds of 80 mph.

*Coordinated Universal Time: all subsequent references to time will be in UTC.

Though diminished in strength by landfall in Florida, once back over water Katrina regained hurricane status at 0600 with maximum sustained winds of 75 mph. Instead of traveling west as forecasted, the storm moved south, almost parallel to the coastline of densely populated Miami. Katrina continued on its path through Coral Gables and southwest Miami, traveled southwest through the unpopulated Everglades National Park and, again diminished in intensity, exited the state near the southern tip of mainland Florida.

On 26 August at 0900, Tropical Storm Katrina entered the Gulf of Mexico. The upper-level flow and warm surface temperatures, coupled with the low wind shear of the Gulf, allowed the storm to quickly strengthen. An hour later, Katrina was upgraded to hurricane status once again. The storm underwent two periods of expansion between 26 and 28 August. The first period involved an increase in maximum sustained winds from 75 to 110 mph in a twenty-four-hour period ending 0600, 27 August. An eye became visible in infrared satellite imagery early on 27 August, and Katrina became a Category 3 hurricane with 115 mph winds at 1200 about 365 miles southeast of the Mississippi River. Katrina nearly doubled in size on 27 August, and by the end of the day, tropical storm force winds extended up to 140 miles from the center. As it churned westward on 27 August, it produced tropical storm force winds and heavy rainfall over portions of Cuba. The new eyewall contracted into a sharply defined ring by 0000, 28 August, and a second expansion occurred.

Katrina grew from a low-end Category 3 to a Category 5 hurricane in less than twelve hours with winds reaching an intensity of 167 mph at 1200, 28 August. Once the storm reached Category 3 intensity, it began an eyewall replacement cycle, which disrupted the maximum sustainable wind speeds within. This cycle lasted nearly eighteen hours and allowed the size to almost double. The hurricane continued along on its west-southwest path over the water, eventually overcoming this temporary weakness. The wind speeds had increased to 145 mph, and Katrina was upgraded to a Category 4 hurricane at 0540, 28 August. A path shift, which occurred as the storm overcame the shelf of the Gulf, now had Katrina advancing across the water, targeted to make landfall on the Louisiana coast. It was now moving on a west-northwest path at about 8 mph. Powerful hurricane winds reached 70 miles from the eye, and tropical storm force winds blew as far as 160 miles from the eye.

By 1200, the maximum sustained winds had grown to 160 mph, thus upgrading the storm from a Category 4 hurricane to a Category 5 hurricane with potentially catastrophic consequences. Katrina continued along a north-northwest path at 12 mph and was 250 miles from the mouth of the Mississippi River. The storm was certain to land there if it continued on that path. Hurricane strength winds reached up to 85 miles from the eye of the hurricane, and tropical storm force winds were sustained up to 185 miles from the center. The central pressure continued to drop until it reached 908 mb, enabling both the velocity of the winds and the extended reach of its winds to be maintained.

At 1800, Katrina reached peak intensity. Winds roared at a maximum sustained speed of 175 mph, with gusts of up to 215 mph. Winds of hurricane force extended up to 105 miles from the center, and tropical storm force winds reached up to 205 miles from the eye. The central pressure also dropped slightly to 902 mb. It continued along its path to land, still targeted at the Gulf Coast states from Morgan City, Louisiana, to the Florida/Alabama border; however, a slight change of direction took place as Katrina began to head in a northwest direction at almost 13 mph.

At 2100 of the same day, Katrina's center was located approximately 150 miles south of the mouth of the Mississippi River, and the central pressure stood at 902 mb. The storm roared on at 13 mph on a northwestern course. Conditions had started to deteriorate by this point due to an eyewall-replacement cycle. This cycle caused the storm to deteriorate much faster than was expected because the inner eyewall broke down before the outer eyewall was able to strengthen enough to support the rest of the hurricane. The maximum sustained winds dropped to 165 mph, but it remained a Category 5 hurricane. Winds of minimal hurricane force spread out up to 105 miles from the center of the storm, and winds of tropical storm force reached out to 230 miles. Tropical storm force winds were sustained along the coast of southeast Louisiana and the mouth of the Mississippi.

The new eyewall that formed late on 27 August began to erode on its southern side late on 28 August. These structural changes likely contributed to the rapid weakening that was observed prior to final landfall. On 28 August, Katrina made a gradual turn toward the northwest and north and the central Gulf Coast. During this period, the storm's wind field expanded considerably with hurricane force winds extending about 125 miles from the center and tropical storm force winds 230 miles. At 0540 Hurricane Katrina reached Category 4 with 145 mph winds, and by 1200 it was a Category 5 storm with maximum sustained winds of 175 mph, gusts of up to 215 mph, and a central pressure of 902 mb.

In a press conference at roughly 1500, New Orleans Mayor Ray Nagin, with Louisiana Governor Kathleen Blanco at his side, declared that "a mandatory evacuation order is hereby called for all of the parishes of Orleans . . . we're facing the storm most of us have feared."

Following Nagin's speech, Governor Blanco stated that President Bush had called her immediately before the press conference. Bush had told her he was "concerned about the [storm's] impact" and to "please ensure that there would be a mandatory evacuation of New Orleans." Katrina was expected to make landfall overnight.

Shortly after the meeting, the National Weather Service issued a bulletin predicting devastating damage. At 1700, the Louisiana Superdome was opened as a "refuge of last resort" for those residents who were unable to obtain safe transport out of the city. President Bush declared a state of emergency in Alabama and Mississippi and a major disaster in Florida under the authority of the Stafford Act.

At this point, the National Hurricane Center officially shifted the possible track of Katrina from the Florida Panhandle to the Mississippi/Louisiana coast. Governor Blanco declared a state of emergency for the state of Louisiana. The declaration included activation of Louisiana's emergency response and recovery program under the command of the director of the state office of Homeland Security and Emergency Preparedness. Following the declaration of a state of emergency, federal troops were deployed to Louisiana to coordinate the planning of operations with FEMA.

Early on 29 August Katrina turned northward toward the ridge over Florida. The storm then made landfall as a Category 3 hurricane with estimated maximum sustained winds of 127 mph near Buras, Louisiana at 1110.

By 1300 water was seen rising on both sides of the Industrial

Canal in New Orleans. At approximately 1314, the New Orleans office of the National Weather Service issued a flash flood warning for Orleans Parish and St. Bernard Parish, citing a levee breach at the Industrial Canal. The National Weather Service predicted three to eight feet of water and advised people in the warning area to move to higher ground immediately. By 2100, there were six to eight feet of water in the Lower Ninth Ward. At 1500, Katrina made its third landfall near Pearlington, Mississippi, with sustained winds of 120 mph. By 1600, there were approximately ten feet of water in St. Bernard Parish.

At 1900, New Orleans officials confirmed a breach of the 17th Street Canal levee. There was also confirmation of breaches at two other canals. In a press conference, New Orleans Homeland Security Director Terry Ebbert stated that he was positive there were casualties resulting from the storm, based on calls to emergency workers from people trapped in trees and homes. He said that everybody who had a way or wanted to get out of the way of the storm did so. For those who did not, it might likely be their last night on this earth.

Police were fanning out across the city to assess damage, rescue people, and get a good grasp of the situation before nightfall. The hardest-hit areas of the city were the Lower Ninth Ward, New Orleans East, Gentilly, Lakeview, St. Bernard Parish, and Plaquemines Parish. Governor Blanco ordered sixty-eight school buses into New Orleans from surrounding parishes to begin evacuating any survivors who remained in the city. FEMA Director Michael Brown also urged local fire and rescue departments outside Louisiana, Alabama, and Mississippi not to send trucks or emergency workers into disaster areas without an explicit request for help from state or local governments. Brown sought the approval from Homeland Security Secretary Michael Chertoff five hours after landfall to dispatch one thousand Homeland Security workers into the region. Brown acknowledged that this process would take two days. He described Katrina as a "near catastrophic event." Brown defined the roles of requested assigned personnel and additional aid from the United States Department of Homeland Security:

> Establish and maintain positive working relationships with
> disaster affected communities and the citizens of those

communities. Collect and disseminate information and make referrals for appropriate assistance. Identify potential issues within the community and report to appropriate personnel. Convey a positive image of disaster operations to government officials, community organizations, and the general public. Perform outreach with community leaders on available Federal disaster assistance.

President Bush declared Louisiana, Mississippi, and Alabama major disaster areas under the authority of the Stafford Act.

Katrina remained extremely large as it weakened and moved inland over southern and central Mississippi, becoming a Category 1 hurricane by 1800, 29 August. It weakened to a tropical storm about six hours later just northwest of Meridian, Mississippi. Katrina accelerated on 30 August, between the ridge over the southeastern United States and an eastward-moving trough over the Great Lakes. It turned northeast over the Tennessee Valley and became a tropical depression at 1200, 30 August. The depression continued northeast and subsided into a low-pressure system by 0000, 31 August. The system was absorbed within a frontal zone later that day over the eastern Great Lakes.

Katrina produced sixty-two tornadoes in eight states from Florida to Pennsylvania. The highest total recorded rainfall from Katrina was 16.33 inches in Perrine, Florida; Big Branch, Louisiana, recorded 14.92 inches of rainfall, the highest rainfall amount in Louisiana. The highest measured wind gust during Katrina was 135 mph, recorded in Popularville, MS, at the Pearl River County Emergency Operations Center before the instrument failed. Katrina produced wind gusts of 80 to 110 mph well inland over portions of southern, central, and eastern Mississippi. The highest reported wind gust in inland Mississippi was 114 mph in Ellisville. The strongest official sustained wind in Louisiana during Katrina was 87 mph, measured at the Grand Isle Coastal Marine Automated Network station. The lowest observed pressure was 920.2 mb at the University of Louisiana-Monroe Weather Station in Buras. Storm-surge data indicates that the maximum surge was twenty-six to twenty-eight feet along the coast of Mississippi. Damage survey data suggests that the surge penetrated at least six miles inland in many portions of coastal Mississippi. The estimated storm surge in southeast Louisiana near New Orleans was ten to fifteen feet and was ten to twelve feet along the coast of Alabama. Four levee breaches occurred around New Orleans on August 29: two along the London Avenue Canal, one along the 17th Street Canal, and one along the Industrial Canal.

The devastation Katrina left over southeast Louisiana and coastal Mississippi was immense. The levee breaches and overtopping resulted in floodwaters of fifteen to twenty feet, covering about 80% of the city. The catastrophic damage and loss of life inflicted by this hurricane was staggering, with an estimated 1,353 direct fatalities and 275,000 homes damaged or destroyed. According to the American Insurance Services Group, Katrina caused an estimated $40.6 billion in insured losses (as of June 2006). The National Hurricane Center typically doubles the estimated insured losses for an estimate of total damage losses in the U.S., giving a total of $81.2 billion in damage. Tens of thousands of jobs were lost due to severely damaged or destroyed businesses and supporting infrastructure. Major highways in and around New Orleans were damaged or destroyed, disrupting commerce. Katrina also affected the oil and gas industry by damaging platforms, shutting down refineries, and interrupting operations at two major U.S. ports in Louisiana. Total economic losses could be greater than $100 billion. These impacts make Katrina the most costly hurricane in U.S. history and one of the five deadliest hurricanes to ever strike the U.S.

Early Images of Katrina

26 August 1715—Katrina rages across Florida

28 August 1545—Strengthened Katrina poised off coast

29 August 1415—Katrina finds land in southern Louisiana

29 August 1615—Katrina targets Mississippi Coast

30 August 1315—Weakened Katrina tracks to the north

Eye wall of Katrina taken from aircraft

Eye wall of Katrina taken from aircraft

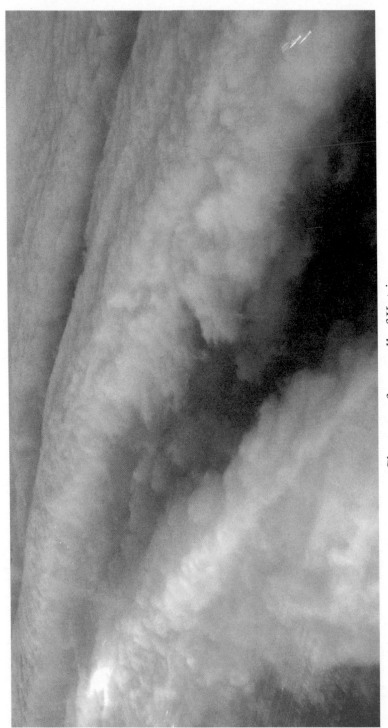

Close-up of eye wall of Katrina

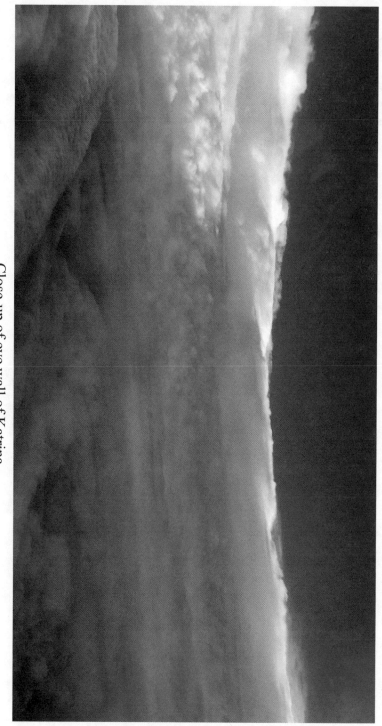

Close-up of eye wall of Katrina

The Grey Ghost Lingers: Katrina and Louisiana

New Orleans—a city known for its parades, jazz funerals, cuisine, tourism, sports, and friendly spirit—was set back decades on the morning of 29 August when Hurricane Katrina made landfall on the Gulf Coast between the major cities of New Orleans and Mobile, Alabama. Since that day, these areas have been struggling to recapture the physical nature of what they were and the spirit of what they are.

Hurricane Katrina made landfall in the Gulf Coast region as a Category 3 hurricane with storm-surge winds of a Category 5 hurricane. By 30 August, 80% of the city of New Orleans was flooded, with some areas submerged by twenty feet of water.

Population

Historians will agree that the people are the essence of New Orleans. Their accents, history, camaraderie, pride, and presence are key components of the city's richness. According to the United States Census Bureau, the estimated population for Orleans Parish in 2005 before Katrina hit was 454,863. After being struck by the storm, which brought with it wind damage and flooding, the population was vastly diminished. Orleans Parish was estimated to have a population of 150,000 in January of 2006; 196,000 in May.

An estimated 9.7 million people living in Alabama, Louisiana, and Mississippi experienced hurricane force winds as Katrina slammed into the Gulf Coast. From the three states that were affected by the storm, 300,000 displaced people came from Orleans Parish alone. Many of these 300,000 people are reported to have been poor, with 30% having incomes 1.5% below the poverty level. Of those displaced, about 44% were African Americans. 88,000 were elderly, and 183,000 were public-school-age children.

As a result of Katrina, New Orleans' population was

redistributed across the Southern United States. Houston, Texas, had an increase of 35,000 people; Mobile, Alabama, over 24,000; Baton Rouge, Louisiana, over 15,000; and Hammond, Louisiana, over 10,000, nearly doubling its size. Chicago, Illinois, received over 6,000 people, the most of any non-southern city.

◇◇

Jackie Gresham, owner of TAT-2, a tattoo parlor in the Lower Ninth Ward, owns a two-story house, with a second-floor balcony, complete with ceiling fan and wrought-iron railings, New Orleans trademarks. Paul Ruffin interviewed her in December of 2005, just after the Lower Ninth was opened up to traffic.

I've been in this place twenty-five years. This is the first neighborhood tattoo shop around here. Was. I lost a lot of my art stuff during Katrina—papers, references and stuff like that—but I got my Brown Fairy Book *back, and I'm ready to roll. We're waiting to see what happens to these houses, but I'm gonna tell you, the system doesn't help you. My house was pretty solid, but a city bulldozer knocked a hole in it when they were clearing the street. I am beginning to think that it might be best just to bulldoze all this down. I hate to be the one to say it. Let me tell you why. Because . . . you know how much it cost to build this house? My whole upstairs is fine. I got hardwood floors, new cabinets. Everybody's talking about the mold and getting sick. I don't think you can get that out of here. I'm just gonna clean out my house and basically see what*  *happens. I don't think anybody in their right mind is going to come back in here and rebuild. Construction is expensive these days, even if you're doing it yourself. I mean, I love this house*

NOAA ADVISORY 0500 UTC

...POTENTIALLY CATASTROPHIC CATEGORY FIVE HURRICANE KATRINA CONTINUES TO APPROACH THE NORTHERN GULF COAST... ...SUSTAINED HURRICANE-FORCE WINDS NEARING THE SOUTHEASTERN LOUISIANA COAST...

AT 0500 UTC THE CENTER OF HURRICANE KATRINA WAS LOCATED NEAR LAT 27.9N... LONG 89.5W OR ABOUT 90 MILES SOUTH-SOUTHWEST OF THE MOUTH OF THE MISSISSIPPI RIVER AND ABOUT 150 MILES SOUTH-SOUTHEAST OF NEW ORLEANS.

KATRINA IS MOVING TOWARD THE NORTH-NORTHWEST NEAR 10 MPH...AND A TURN TO THE NORTH IS EXPECTED OVER THE NEXT 12 TO 24 HOURS. ON THE FORECAST TRACK THE CENTER OF THE HURRICANE WILL BE VERY NEAR THE NORTHERN GULF COAST MONDAY MORNING. HOWEVER... CONDITIONS ARE ALREADY DETERIORATING ALONG PORTIONS OF THE CENTRAL AND NORTHEASTERN GULF COAST...AND WILL CONTINUE TO WORSEN THROUGH THE NIGHT.

MAX SUSTAINED WINDS REMAIN NEAR 160 MPH WITH HIGHER GUSTS. HURRICANE FORCE WINDS EXTEND OUTWARD UP TO 105 MILES FROM THE CENTER...AND TROPICAL STORM FORCE WINDS EXTEND OUTWARD UP TO 230 MILES. A WIND GUST TO 98 MPH WAS RECENTLY REPORTED FROM SOUTHWEST PASS LOUISIANA.

COASTAL STORM SURGE FLOODING OF 18 TO 22 FT ABOVE NORMAL TIDE LEVELS... LOCALLY AS HIGH AS 28 FT...ALONG WITH LARGE AND DANGEROUS BATTERING WAVES...CAN BE EXPECTED NEAR AND TO THE EAST OF WHERE THE CENTER MAKES LANDFALL. SOME LEVEES IN THE GREATER NEW ORLEANS AREA COULD BE OVERTOPPED. SIGNIFICANT STORM SURGE FLOODING WILL OCCUR ELSEWHERE ALONG THE CENTRAL AND NORTHEASTERN GULF OF MEXICO COAST.

RAINFALL TOTALS OF 5 TO 10 INCHES... WITH ISOLATED MAXIMUM AMOUNTS OF 15 INCHES...ARE POSSIBLE ALONG THE PATH OF KATRINA

and this town, but I was planning on going to Mississippi to retire anyway. Was. Until this storm came along. You know, you want to be part of the rebuilding. I'm helping out. And if these people need tattoos, I got'm. No problem. And they seem to need them. Business is doing fairly well down here. I was stunned. People come back and look at their property and somehow want to get a tattoo on their way out. Don't ask me why.

◇◇◇◇◇◇◇◇◇◇◇◇◇◇◇◇◇◇◇◇◇◇◇◇

Lower Ninth Ward

While the Lower Ninth Ward has been a famous area in New Orleans since its establishment in 1852, its renown soared on 29 August 2005, when it became famous all over again, but this time the reason was catastrophic. This area, known for its celebrated musicians, residential structures, and rich culture, is now nationally recognized for its tragic devastation in the aftermath of Hurricane Katrina.

One of the lowest points in the city, the Lower Ninth is located between the mouth of the Mississippi River to the south and the Saint Bernard

Parish to the east. The neighborhood, 1.2 miles from east to west and two miles from north to south, is the largest ward geographically of the seventeen wards that comprise New Orleans. This small vicinity was the most devastated in the city. Hurricane Katrina's storm surge flooded even the highest areas of the Lower Ninth. The force of the water not only flooded homes but smashed and knocked many off of their foundations with the help of a large barge, ING4727. This barge came into the neighborhood through a breech near Claiborne Avenue, leveling homes as it floated on the floodwaters.

In 2000, the population of the Lower Ninth Ward was 14,008 persons, 98.3% being African-American. The low cost of housing served to concentrate the population of poor, working class laborers. According to the 2000 US Census, the Lower Ninth Ward had a poverty level of 36.4%, with a quarter of households having an annual income of less than $10,000 and half living on less than $20,000. Although the population is mostly lower class, the neighborhood prides itself on being one of the few areas in the city without housing projects. Furthermore, 60% of the homes in the area were owner occupied, the highest rate of home ownership in New Orleans. Peter Wagner and Susan Edwards point out in "New Orleans by the Number" on the Dollars and Sense website that before Hurricane Katrina, the Lower Ninth "was actually a shining example of Bush's often touted 'ownership society.'"

◇◇◇

Another report from Paul Ruffin (December 2005):

> B.F. is not smiling as she helps her husband unload furniture and carry it into her mother-in-law's place—the right side of a wooden duplex, painted blue, with red Xs on both sides showing that no bodies had been found there. The place has obviously been in deep water, there is no structural damage, just lots of trash about the place and ankle-deep mud and sludge everywhere. B.F. says that she went to a hotel downtown, and after the storm passed, she and others were headed back down into their neighborhood when the levees broke.
>
> *Water was everywhere. Looked like the Mississippi had*

done been rerouted through the Ninth Ward. You could see the tops of some of the taller houses, but most was completely underwater. Lots of folks that we seen was screaming and hollering, there was dead bodies turning up, and people was squealing and hollering when they came off that bridge. I mean, they were falling all over the ground. It was just . . . . There's houses on top of houses, cars on top of houses. It's sad for me. I mean, it's a lot of people that died, and they still finding bodies, you know.

All buildings in the Lower Ninth bore the familiar X.

Percent of Population
Home Owners

	Total Population	Blacks
United States	66%	49%
Louisiana	68%	53%
New Orleans	47%	43%
Lower Ninth Ward	59%	57%

Source: US Census

Percent of population
Place of residence, 5 years ago

	Born in the state they live in now	In same house	In same county/ parish	In same state
United States	60%	54%	79%	89%
Louisiana	79%	59%	84%	93%
New Orleans	77%	57%	85%	91%
Lower Ninth Ward	92%	74%	97%	98%

Source: US Census

Economic Effects

Economists may disagree about the amount and duration of national economic change following Hurricane Katrina; however, they all agree that the impact on the economy will introduce a season of uncertainty. Before the hurricane, the region supported approximately 1 million non-farm jobs, with 600,000 of them in New Orleans.

Douglas Holtz-Eakin, Director of the Congressional Budget Office, points out that the "unemployment rate had been falling steadily. The economy had added 150,000-200,000 jobs a month." He goes on to state how the effects of Katrina will "significantly affect the growth path of the US economy." Daniel Gross supports the comments of the CBO director in his article "The Katrina Premium" by writing the following: "The hurricane directly affected only a small chunk of the consumer economy. Louisiana and Mississippi have a combined population of 7.5 million and account for about 2 percent of the nation's economic activity. But it will indirectly affect all consumers and businesses, in the United States and abroad." While neither man foresees a recession, the change will be noticeable enough for the country to realize how important New Orleans and its surrounding areas are to our economic stability.

The problem is that New Orleans lies at the heavily trafficked intersection of the Old and New Economies. The region's economy is based on agriculture, water transport, and natural resources. But moving and selling goods requires an intricate web of supply chains, pipelines, and commercial arteries that connect producers to consumers. The networked economy is not about just bytes and fiber-optic cable—it is about oil, grain, and sugar. And when the infrastructure of these networks gets damaged, it cannot be replaced easily or cheaply. If New Orleans were pure Old Economy—if, for example, it simply grew wheat—its devastation would not cost that much because other wheat and grain growers would replace it. If it were pure New Economy, like Wall Street, it could bounce back instantly because its real assets (information and people) would not be irretrievably lost. But because it is right in the middle, the damage will be enormous.

Professor Richardson, an economist from the hard-hit areas, supports the statements above. He takes the time to cite a few examples:

> In the New Orleans metropolitan area there are a number of sectors—one being the petrochemical sector, the oil industry; there is also shipbuilding, Avondale shipbuilding grounds. And you have the Lockheed Martin space shuttle area. And then you have four private universities plus the public university. And then of course your tourist industry is a large part of the economy as well.

While reconstruction will bring a boost to the construction industry and its suppliers, economists warn that this will not increase economic activity as a whole. The money for rebuilding will be diverted from money which would have been spent in other areas. *The Broken Window Fallacy*, by Henry Hazlitt, detailing what happens when a vandal breaks a $250 window, which a storekeeper then has to replace, best describes the economic disparity:

> After all, if windows were never broken, what would happen to the glass business? Then, of course, the thing is endless. The glazier will have $250 more to spend with other merchants, and these in turn will have $250 to spend with still other merchants, and so ad infinitum. The smashed window will go on providing money and employment in ever-widening circles. The logical conclusion from all this would be . . . that

the little hoodlum who threw the brick, far from being a public menace, was a public benefactor.

The crowd is correct in realizing that the local glass shop will benefit from this act of vandalism. They have not considered, however, that the shopkeeper would have spent the $250 on something else if he did not have to replace the window. He might have been saving that money for a new set of golf clubs, but since he has now spent the money, he cannot and the golf shop has lost a sale. He might have used the money to purchase new equipment for his business, or to take a vacation, or to purchase new clothing. So the glass store's gain is another store's loss, so there hasn't been a net gain in economic activity. In fact, there has been a decline in the economy.

Instead of [the shopkeeper] having a window and $250, he now has merely a window. Or, as he was planning to buy the suit that very afternoon, instead of having both a window and a suit he must be content with the window or the suit. If we think of him as a part of the community, the community has lost a new suit that might otherwise have come into being, and is just that much poorer.

Employment

The main areas in Louisiana that have experienced prolonged unemployment are New Orleans, Metairie, and Kenner. In a report created by Congressional Budget Office in September of 2005, it was found that "employment for September (2005) will decline significantly—estimates of the impact range from 150,000 to half a million—as a direct consequence of the hurricane."

Before the storm, the region was already one of the poorest in America with one of the highest unemployment rates. Since then, hundreds of thousands of residents of southern Louisiana, including nearly everyone who lived in New Orleans, were left unemployed. No paychecks were being cashed and no money was being spent, and therefore no taxes were being collected by local governments. The lack of revenue will limit the resources of the affected communities and states for years to come. Due to the previous economic state of New Orleans and surrounding areas, Jim Sensenbrenner, Republican chairman of the House Judiciary Committee, refused to allow victims of the hurricane to take advantage of any exception to the recent Bankruptcy Reform, a bill passed with

> **IMPACT BREAKDOWN**
> - **1,101 confirmed dead; more still unaccounted for**
> - **More than 1.4 million registrations for federal assistance**
> - **More than 280,000 housing units destroyed**
> - **40,446 federally funded temporary housing units occupied**

widespread support of the banking industry that aims to curb abuse of bankruptcy protection by repeat filers and those who are able to repay debts reasonably. However, reports do provide an inkling of hope. Employment was predicted by the Congressional Budget Office to increase in subsequent months, as workers return home and businesses reopen and as reconstruction activity gathers steam.

Energy and Oil Production

Chief economist with Action Economics, Michael Englund, said it best: "It is all about oil." If Americans felt the wrath of Katrina in no other area, they would see results in the gas and energy arenas. Hurricane Katrina shut down 91% of production in the Gulf Region, and 83% of gas production was halted due to damage to refineries and rigs. "Nine of the region's 14 refineries are shut, representing 12.5 percent of U.S. refining capacity," according to the *Financial Times*. The region makes up a fourth of the US oil and gas production, which explains why Americans were paying $3 per gallon at the pump rather than $1.86, as they had a year ago. Englund continues: "Without the hurricane we had perceived a bounce in U.S. oil inventory. But if refineries are out of commission because of damage or flooding for an unspecified period of time, it will shock the entire system and I expect firms will hold back their production."

The storm interrupted oil production, importation, and refining in the Gulf area and thus produced a major effect on fuel prices. Before the storm, one-tenth of all the crude oil consumed in the United States and almost half of the gasoline produced in the country came from refineries in the Gulf states. An additional 24% of the natural gas supply is extracted or imported in the region. The nation's Strategic Petroleum Reserve is also stored there.

Power outages in the wake of Katrina caused distribution problems for oil and natural gas. Pipelines that move petroleum products from places like Houston to areas of the east coast had their flows interrupted because power outages shut down the pumps that kept materials flowing.

At 0700 on 29 August Ted Falgout, Port Director of Port Fourchon, a key oil and gas hub 60 miles south of New Orleans on the Gulf of Mexico, reported that the port had taken a direct hit from the hurricane. The port services approximately 16% of the nation's supply of crude oil and natural gas. According to Falgout, Hurricane Katrina "will impact oil and gas infrastructure, not just short term but long term as well. The impact of the storm—the Gulf is shut down; all of the area of the storm is shut down; a half billion dollars a day of oil and gas is unavailable."

The Louisiana Offshore Oil Port, which imports 11% of all US oil consumption, closed on 27 August, and Shell reported a reduction in production of 420,000 barrels per day. The port was undamaged by the storm and resumed operation within hours of getting power back.

Due to fears that the production of oil in the United States would be cut by up to one-third of normal capacity, the price of oil fluctuated greatly. West Texas Intermediate crude oil futures reached a record high of over $70 per barrel. There were many reports to Louisiana authorities and elsewhere of price gouging, not only for gasoline, but also for other needed items, such as bottled water. In some areas, gasoline was being sold for as much as $6 per gallon. Just before the storm, average fuel prices were approximately $2.50 per US gallon.

Long lines developed at some gas stations throughout the U.S. as customers rushed to buy gasoline, anticipating price increases in the wake of the storm. Emphasizing the seriousness of the situation and in light of similar incidents in his own state, Governor Mike Easley of North Carolina issued a statement asking all North Carolinians to conserve fuel and limit non-essential road trips, and he urged state employees to car-pool. On the day of the Governor's announcement, many gas stations around the state ran out of fuel, and long lines formed at others.

By 1200 on 31 August eight Gulf refineries remained shut down, and one was operating at reduced capacity. Evaluation of five of the eight refineries was delayed due to limited access. Aside from the problems involved in restarting the refineries (which is a lengthy process) there were additional major issues with worker housing, since the hurricane destroyed a large proportion of homes.

The Environmental Protection Agency moved to reduce prices by temporarily lifting fuel standards in America until 15 September. Crude oil was released from the Strategic Petroleum Reserve to combat prices, for if prices remained high for a long period of time, it would lead to a decrease in consumer spending and cause many foreign economies, especially in Asia, to suffer. President Bush also temporarily waived the Jones Act, allowing foreign oil companies to ship oil between ports of the United States.

By 7 September, Gulf oil production had returned to 42% of normal. Of the ten refineries that were shut down by Katrina, four were expected to be back at full capacity within a week; however, another four could be out of commission for months.

Agriculture and Trade

Energy is not the only valuable commodity that flows through New Orleans. As the *Wall Street Journal* notes, New Orleans ports "handle roughly half of the corn, wheat and soybeans exported from the U.S., much of which reaches the city on barges traveling on the Mississippi River." Katrina disrupted the vital supply chains that funnel goods from the Midwest to global markets and from global markets to the Midwest. Farmers have been floating grain to external markets on river barges since the 18th century, not because it offers speed but because it is the most economically efficient means of doing so. As the Associated Press notes, "The Mississippi River is the cheapest route for shipping many crops and other commodities destined for overseas markets." So, farmers looking to get their goods to market will now have to rely on more expensive modes of transport. And importers will either have to absorb higher costs or pass them along to consumers. Before the onset of Hurricane Katrina, approximately 25% of Chiquita's banana imports used to arrive in the United States at the company's Gulfport, Mississippi, facility. No longer. That company, and many others, will have to scramble to find alternate (and, likely, more expensive) arrangements.

Of further consideration: the agricultural staples that are produced in huge volume in the Gulf Coast region and used in a wide range of products in the United States and overseas, such as oysters, chickens, cotton, and sugar. Katrina will have the effect of making them more expensive and set off a scramble among the companies that need steady supplies to find new sources. The shortages will drive up prices here and make their exports more expensive—and less competitive—abroad.

Although small in area, the Gulf Coast offers a lot to every region of the United States and some neighboring countries. The flow of goods along the Mississippi River and through the Port of New Orleans and the Port of South Louisiana was tremendously impacted. A lot of agricultural products are imported to other countries: rice, chicken products, wheat, etc. Jim Richardson, professor of economics and director of the Public Administration Institute at Louisiana State University, adds:

That will have an impact on farmers throughout the Midwest very easily. Coming into the country you have things like steel products, aluminum products, and products of that nature that will have an impact also because most of those products go up the Mississippi River, up to the Midwest and over to the East Coast.

When asked if he would measure the larger impact of Hurricane Katrina on the economy by things like commodity prices, Director of the Congressional Budget Office, Douglas Holtz-Eakin, answered:

I think the petrochemicals and the pace at which natural gas, oil production, the refining and distribution of gasoline, the pace at which that comes back will be the key to the national impacts. The second to look at is the degree to which shipping is restored along the Mississippi and that transportation link, a quarter of all agriculture exports going out that route. Those are things that can be monitored. If it passes relatively quickly, the impacts will be small as a result.

Addressing many of the problems caused by Katrina, Jim Richardson says that reviving the ports is "just a matter of getting the people back—you need to have workers."

Airline Industry

Tourists spent around five billion dollars in New Orleans in the year prior to Hurricane Katrina, representing half of Louisiana's tourism income. Now visitors are switching to other destinations. Businessmen, too, are going elsewhere, as conventions are being moved to cities such as Atlanta. The collapse of New Orleans' tourism took its toll on the airline industry, forcing airlines to cancel dozens of flights to the city's stricken Louis Armstrong airport. Only humanitarian flights were allowed to land.

Although the flight disruption meant a significant loss of revenue, the biggest financial impact on the airlines came from soaring fuel prices because of the oil shutdowns. Daily jet fuel production was down by 13%, and the price has since gone up by 19%. With many US airlines already in trouble, particularly Atlanta-based Delta, energy analysts thought the latest fuel price rise would push some carriers into bankruptcy.

Real Estate

The real estate market and home building industry have been major drivers of the US economy in recent years. The impact of Katrina on those important sectors is difficult to gauge, economists say.

On the one hand, there was a significant fall in interest rates in the wake of the storm that kept mortgage rates low and continued to support home prices and building around the country. However, the demand for goods for rebuilding could cause shortages and price spikes for some goods, according to economists in the sector. The problem could have been worsened by the fact that many imported building materials that entered the country entered through the recently closed Gulf ports.

Destroyed Churches
- 35 churches affected
- 17 seriously damaged

Reconstruction

The road towards reconstruction will be one that continues for years and years. Some predict that the cities will never be the same. The people may return, the spirit may be renewed, but there will always be something missing. The physical rebuilding of the cities will involve many components. The Congressional Budget Office outlines these dimensions as "the rebuilding of residences, businesses, infrastructure, and stocks of consumer durables." The gross domestic product increases 0.2% with every 100,000 housing units that are rebuilt. This number does not include the nonresidential structures, which have a tremendous effect on the GDP, for it is about "90% as large as the stock of residential fixed assets."

While the effects of Hurricane Katrina linger, consumers face further hikes in gasoline prices, shortages in the supermarkets, and the prospect of bankruptcies in the airline industry. In the areas that bore the brunt of the storm, relief experts say reconstruction efforts could take longer than in previous emergencies, with the most impoverished inhabitants likely to be last in the queue for resources. Insurance companies predict that Hurricane Katrina will turn out to be the costliest US storm in history, with an estimated total of $25 billion in damages, overtaking the $21 billion of insured losses inflicted by Hurricane Andrew in 1992.

As of April 2006, the Bush Administration had sought $105 billion for repairs and reconstruction in the region, not accounting for damage to the economy caused by potential interruption of the oil supply, destruction of the Gulf Coast's highway infrastructure, and exports of commodities such as grain. While the numbers are being crunched and checks are being written, the timing of rebuilding still remains uncertain. In September 2005, it was reported that reconstruction was to immediately initiate in the areas that suffered the heaviest amount of flooding. However, it was to be delayed several months in New Orleans.

Hurricane Katrina will have substantial and long-term effects on the economies of southern Louisiana and Mississippi. But, given that those two states account for just 2% of total U.S. gross domestic product, the effects on the national economy will be much less dramatic than the effects on the region. Economists predict that, as a result of the storm, national economic growth will be 0.5%-1.0% slower than in the second half of 2005. However, as economic activity recovered in the affected region and rebuilding began, growth has been more rapid than was previously forecast.

Images of Katrina and Louisiana

Relief effort stifled by flood waters

Thank God for average heroes.

Many people had to save themselves.

Some sat patiently waiting for help to reach them.

These folks are relieved to be saved at last.

How courteous of this unnamed store to open its doors to the public. Can't fit what you need into a shopping cart? Help yourself to a pallet-jack.

Shot of devastation of Ninth Ward taken from atop Industrial Canal levee at site of breach.

Yet another example of Katrina's whimsy: This house was swept across the street, its neighbors spared.

Katrina's weird way of parking

A thick, acidic sludge coated everything.

Signs abounded that children once lived in this childless land.

For citywide tours, please call John or Kim.

Any port in a storm

Most churches came through structurally intact, though everything inside was ruined.

This man attempts to take it all in before fleeing for Alabama, where his wife and newborn baby wait.

Times like these, all that's left is devout patriotism.

Katrina cancels class.

The Disney gang awaits the return of the children.

Even houses in the Lower Ninth that escaped destruction were left with terrible concentrations of mold.

The Lower Ninth was not in the mood for a party.

This large-diameter pipe with welded end-caps floated out of the Industrial Canal and became a battering ram.

Just down from second levee breach in the Lower Ninth Ward

This barge came to rest on the nose of a school bus below the levee breach when the flow reversed. When it broke out of the Industrial Canal, it became a giant battering ram that destroyed large numbers of buildings and vehicles.

After Thirty-Six Years a Big, Bad Lady from the Sea Visits the Coast Again: Katrina and Mississippi

The counterclockwise motion of hurricanes forming in the northern hemisphere, combined with the point of landfall of Katrina, contributed to the most fearsome power of the storm being located in the northeastern quadrant of the storm. As the hurricane circulated over land, it weakened significantly. As it continued to circulate, however, it passed back over the warm waters of the Gulf, strengthening again before passing back over the coasts of Mississippi and Alabama, pummeling them again with great force. Thus, though most casualties occurred on the western side of the hurricane, the eastern side was the most forceful. This is the section of Katrina that assaulted the coasts of Mississippi and Alabama. Had the levees in New Orleans not failed, one might reasonably assert that the casualties in Mississippi and Alabama would have greatly outnumbered those in Louisiana.

0700

By 0700, hurricane force winds were battering the coasts of Mississippi and Louisiana. In 1969, Category 5 Hurricane Camille had winds that, though stronger than those of Katrina at landfall, reached up to 75 miles from the center of the storm, while Katrina's winds stretched up to 103 miles from its center, causing serious damage across an enormous swath.

As Katrina made its second landfall at the border of Mississippi and Louisiana on 28 August, wind speeds there were around 125 mph. In Biloxi, east of the impact, wind gusts were recorded at 90 mph. The heaviest impact of the storm in Mississippi was at Gulfport, which was located in the dangerous right-front quadrant of the storm when Katrina reached the Coast. The Gulfport Emergency Operations Center reported sustained winds of 94 mph and gusts of

100 mph. Some of the damages caused by these intense winds were fallen trees, road blockages, and downed traffic lights and power lines. Houses and buildings were also hit with windblown trees and other debris. 75% of the buildings in the city suffered major roof damage, and in many cases roofs were completely torn away. Roof damage was among the chief concerns in Pascagoula, where the Jackson County Emergency Management Agency had to move to the courthouse because the roof of their downtown building came off. In Gulfport, the Gulf Coast Medical Center had to evacuate patients to Alabama hospitals when wind damage resulted in power loss, and significant damage was done to Memorial Hospital. While many other Mississippi hospitals had to evacuate patients due to loss of power, the Ocean Springs Hospital remained open for emergencies. Memorial Hospital in Biloxi suffered major wind damage and broken windows.

0900

The C-MAN station's anemometer at Grand Isle, Louisiana, measured the strongest sustained wind of 86 mph before failing at 0900, two hours before the eyewall made its closest pass.

Rainfall totals of eight to ten inches fell across southwestern Mississippi. Central and northern Mississippi experienced from four to eight inches as the storm continued on its track northward into the Tennessee Valley.

1300

Katrina's storm surge measured twice that of Camille's and impacted 93,000 square miles across 138 parishes and counties. This was not one solid wall of water but worse: a slow, ever-growing surge of water inland that took with it everything in its path. Homes and businesses became little more than concrete slabs commemorating the life that once was.

A massive storm surge swept across open water and collided with the Mississippi coast at 0800. Authorities assert that the majority of deaths caused by Katrina in Mississippi was due to storm-surge flooding in the southernmost counties along the coast. This surge pushed riverboat casinos on shore, in many cases mowing down homes and businesses, some of vast historic import.

Along with the immense economic influence felt along the coast of Mississippi in the wake of tremendous storm-surge flooding of Hurricane Katrina came serious geological impact. Virtually all the coastal islands endured beachfront erosion. Roads and homes were covered with sand, while many homes and businesses that were once ocean-side were ocean-immersed.

With the geological impact came ecological implications. Satellite photos show thousands of acres of coastal wetlands that were submerged due to storm-surge flooding. Though NOAA's weather advisories consistently assured those regions affected by Katrina's storm surge that waters would subside throughout the remainder of the day and into the night, in many sensitive ecological areas it did not and has not. The loss of thousands of acres of coastal wetlands has drastically affected indigenous wildlife. Guardsmen posted in the areas ravaged by Katrina reported that they rarely see gulls and alligators anymore. The Coastal Change Analysis Program undertook a vast land-cover analysis of the Gulf of Mexico in 2001 in an effort to monitor changes in these habitats.

Shortly after Hurricane Katrina, the C-CAP studied an area spanning from Louisiana through Mississippi to Alabama, a space of 47,000 square miles. According to their website, approximately 935 square miles of open water that was not present in the 2001 land-cover study was identified.

A precise measurement of Katrina's storm-surge flooding is difficult to ascertain due to the widespread failure of tide gauges in the northern Gulf of Mexico. In addition, many structures, including businesses and homes, were destroyed along the coast, leaving it virtually impossible to determine the water level based on still-water marks. Despite this, FEMA estimates storm-surge flooding at 24 to 28 feet across a twenty-mile swath centered at Bay St. Louis. This includes the eastern half of Hancock County and the western half of Harrison county, the communities Bay St. Louis, Waveland, Pass Christian, and Long Beach. Data also indicates that the storm surge was 17 to 22 feet along the eastern half of the Mississippi coast from Gulf Port to Pascagoula. The surge penetrated up to six miles inland in most places and up to twelve miles along rivers and bays crossing I-10 in many places.

In an interview with Michael Dunican, Thomas Butera said that he and some friends attempted to ride out Hurricane Katrina in his parents' house in Ocean Springs, Mississippi. The group, which consisted of four young men, all in their early twenties, was tracking the storm via television. This is Thomas Butera's account of that dreadful morning:

At 2 a.m. the power goes out, and the last we know is that the storm is headed for New Orleans.

I wake up around 4:30 a.m., look down at the beach, and see the white caps of the ocean rising up over the road, but I'm thinking it's no big deal, it's happened before, and I go back to sleep.

Around 5:30 a.m. my buddy wakes us all up, scream-ing. Water, about five feet deep, has surrounded the house and debris is crashing up against it.

We collect all our valuables—family photos, records, my guitar—and throw them up in the attic. We even toss the two cats up there.

By this point, the water is so high that you can see and feel the floor move with the waves.

We stuff a double-wide mattress that floats up in the at-tic to sleep on and in case we need to raft out of there.

We hop up into the attic and watch through the windows as the water continues to rise—it's like being in an aquarium.

The front of the house collapses, the doors bust loose, and the windows shatter, water is coming through my living room in three-foot swells and it keeps rising.

The house starts to vibrate like an accordion. We're think-ing it's coming down and know we have to get out.

We jump down into the living room, the water is chest high, though it's hard to judge with the swells, and we ready the raft.

As a joke, we had prepared a little hurricane kit with rope, bandages and a knife—it wasn't funny now that we needed it.

We tie ourselves together with the rope, grab onto the mattress and pray to God that it floats. To me, it feels like jumping off a building and hoping you can fly.

We're getting the shit kicked out of us by all the debris—if there isn't something banging you up top, then it's tearing at you from underneath.

The water smells like petrol and is impossible to keep out of our mouths, it carries us toward the tree-line, which is a collection of debris—houses, outhouses, boats, and cars.

We realize it's suicide to stay with the mattress and kick to a tree.

I cut the rope with the knife and tie it to the tree. We use it to climb up. We keep the mood light with stories and jokes.

NOAA ADVISORY 1100 UTC

...EXTREMELY DANGEROUS CATEGORY FOUR HURRICANE KATRINA PREPARING TO MOVE ONSHORE NEAR SOUTHERN PLAQUEMINES PARISH LOUISIANA... ...HURRICANE-FORCE WIND GUSTS OCCURRING OVER MOST OF SOUTHEASTERN LOUISIANA...IN THE NEW ORLEANS METROPOLITAN AREA...AND AS FAR EAST AS THE CHANDELEUR ISLANDS...

AT 1100 UTC THE CENTER OF MAJOR HURRICANE KATRINA WAS LOCATED NEAR LAT 29.1N... LONG 89.6W OR ABOUT MIDWAY BETWEEN GRAND ISLE AND THE MOUTH OF THE MISSISSIPPI RIVER. THIS IS ALSO ABOUT 70 MILES SOUTH-SOUTHEAST OF NEW ORLEANS AND ABOUT 95 MILES SOUTH-SOUTHWEST OF BILOXI.

KATRINA IS MOVING TOWARD THE NORTH NEAR 15 MPH... AND THIS MOTION IS FORECAST TO CONTINUE TODAY ....KATRINA WILL MOVE ONSHORE THE SOUTHERN COAST OF PLAQUEMINES PARISH NEAR EMPIRE AND BURAS LOUSIANA WITHIN THE NEXT HOUR...AND REACH THE LOUISIANA-MISSISSIPPI BORDER AREA BY EARLY AFTERNOON.

MAX SUSTAINED WINDS ARE NEAR 145 MPH...WITH HIGHER GUSTS. HURRICANE FORCE WINDS EXTEND OUTWARD UP TO 120 MILES FROM THE CENTER...AND TROPICAL STORM FORCE WINDS EXTEND OUTWARD UP TO 230 MILES. DURING THE PAST HOUR...A SUSTAINED WIND OF 56 MPH WITH A GUST TO 85 MPH WAS REPORTED AT NEW ORLEANS LAKEFRONT AIRPORT... AND A SUSTAINED WIND OF 74 MPH WITH A GUST TO 96 MPH WAS REPORTED AT THE NAVAL AIR STATION IN BELLE CHASSE LOUISIANA.

NOAA BUOY 42040 LOCATED ABOUT 50 MILES EAST OF THE MOUTH OF THE MISSISSIPPI RIVER RECENTLY REPORTED WAVES HEIGHTS OF AT LEAST 47 FT.

RAINFALL TOTALS OF 5 TO 10 INCHES... WITH ISOLATED MAXIMUM AMOUNTS OF 15 INCHES...ARE POSSIBLE ALONG THE PATH OF KATRINA.

NOAA ADVISORY 1300 UTC

...LARGE AND EXTREMELY DANGEROUS CATEGORY FOUR HURRICANE KATRINA POUNDING SOUTHEASTERN LOUISIANA AND SOUTHERN MISSISSIPPI...

AT 1300 UTC THE CENTER OF HURRICANE KATRINA WAS LOCATED NEAR LAT 29.7N... LONG 89.6W OR ABOUT 40 MILES SOUTH-EAST OF NEW ORLEANS AND ABOUT 65 MILES SOUTHWEST OF BILOXI.

KATRINA IS MOVING TOWARD THE NORTH NEAR 15 MPH...AND A GRADUAL TURN TO THE NORTH-NORTHEAST AT A SLIGHTLY FASTER FORWARD SPEED IS EXPECTED OVER THE NEXT 24 HOURS. ON THIS TRACK...THE CENTER WILL BE PASSING JUST TO THE EAST OF NEW ORLEANS DUR-ING THE NEXT FEW HOURS WITH THE WORST OF THE WEATHER FOR THAT CITY OCCURRING OVER THE NEXT COUPLE OF HOURS. THE CENTER IS EXPECTED TO MOVE INTO SOUTHERN MISSISSIPPI LATER TODAY.

MAX SUSTAINED WINDS ARE NEAR 135 MPH...WITH HIGHER GUSTS. HURRICANE FORCE WINDS EXTEND OUTWARD UP TO 125 MILES FROM THE CENTER...AND TROP-ICAL STORM FORCE WINDS EXTEND OUT-WARD UP TO 230 MILES. PASCAGOULA MIS-SISSIPPI CIVIL DEFENSE REPORTED A WIND GUST TO 118 MPH...AND GULFPORT MISSIS-SIPPI EMERGENCY OPERATIONS CENTER REPORTED SUSTAINED WINDS OF 94 MPH WITH A GUST TO 100 MPH. BELLE CHASSE LOUISIANA RECENTLY REPORTED SUS-TAINED WINDS OF 76 MPH WITH A GUST TO 88 MPH. A LITTLE EARLIER...BELLE CHASE REPORTED A GUST TO 105 MPH. NEW OR-LEANS LAKEFRONT AIRPORT RECENTLY REPORTED SUSTAINED WINDS OF 69 MPH WITH A GUST TO 86 MPH.

RAINFALL TOTALS OF 5 TO 10 INCHES... WITH ISOLATED MAXIMUM AMOUNTS OF 15 INCHES...ARE POSSIBLE ALONG THE PATH OF KATRINA

After a few hours, we're all freezing and worried about hypo-thermia, so we jump back into the water, which is about 50 degrees warmer, and use the wooden shin-gles that side my parents' house to crawl against the current.

We make it to my neighbor's house, when we see a giant sea turtle. Now normally you're think-ing, oh, wow, a sea turtle, but we're thinking if there's a giant sea turtle, there could be sharks or alligators, and so we enter through a blown-out window, each curl up on a piece of furniture, and ride out the remainder of the hurricane.

I'm so exhausted, I fall asleep on a dresser, not caring about the knobs and handles digging into my side, nor the fact that it's in the kitchen and not the bedroom, where it belongs.

When I wake up, the water has receded, and my friends have dry blankets and towels. The wind is howling outside and the hurri-cane is still in effect but the surge has past.

Wounded, slightly changed, but alive, we return to my broken home, climb into the attic, thank God, and pass out.

◇◇◇◇◇◇◇◇◇◇◇◇◇◇◇◇◇◇◇◇◇◇◇◇◇◇◇◇◇◇

Water was the principal factor behind Katrina's damage across

the Mississippi coast. Rainfall of about six inches was one contributor to the flood damage, but it was not the main factor. The
storm surge, which surpassed previous high levels set by Hurricane
Camille by five to ten feet in many areas, was considered the most
dangerous element of the
storm in terms of human
fatalities and destruction of
structures and the environ-
ment. Flooding from both
the storm surge and heavy
rainfall caused water damage to the ground levels of
myriad buildings. In some
areas, water levels rose to
more than twenty feet. The
storm surge from Waveland

HUMAN IMPACT
• **231 confirmed dead**
• **5 unidentified dead**
• **67 missing**
• **20,447 Red Cross staff and volunteers
  in Mississippi**
• **5,543,006 Red Cross meals served**
• **42,768 people sheltered by Red Cross**
• **229 Red Cross shelters opened**
• **approx. 100,000 people still living in
  FEMA trailers**

to Long Beach reached levels of nearly twenty-eight feet. Katrina's
maximum official storm-surge mark was 27.8 feet, recorded in Pass
Christian.

Transportation routes were significantly impacted by flooding and displacement of sand and other debris along major roads.
In many places Highway 90 was buried under several feet of sand
moved by the storm surge. The eastbound lanes of I-10 between
Biloxi and Gulfport were blocked by debris. Highway and railroad
bridges leading to Biloxi were completely destroyed. U.S. 49 and
Highway 11 were shut down. Along U.S. 90, sailboats and barges
were washed onto the four-lane highway and into buildings. For
about two weeks following the storm, the traffic along the Mississippi River was below normal capacity, and the Mississippi State
Port lost its lifting facilities and cranes. All that remains of the Bay
St. Louis Bridge are pylons, and other bridges were damaged as
well.

The structural damage from flooding had a vast range of effects, from ground floor flooding to entire neighborhoods washing
away. 80% of the houses and buildings in Waveland were declared
uninhabitable after Katrina's impact. In Gulfport, three firehouses
were heavily damaged, and three of the four walls of Harrison Central 9th Grade School collapsed. Fun Time USA lost everything ex-

cept bumper cars, a pool, and the go-cart track. Along Pass Road, businesses and houses were severely damaged or demolished. Entire homes disappeared from Beach Boulevard. In downtown Gulfport, where streets were under ten feet of water, looting was also a problem.

Whole neighborhoods were washed away by Katrina in Bay St. Louis. An entire Pass Christian harbor and beachfront community was lost due to water damages. On Second Street, a home was displaced by Katrina and left in the middle of the road. The eastern part of Pass Christian was submerged under water that rose twenty feet above ground level. In Long Beach, within about 200 yards of U.S. 90, most of the buildings completely disappeared. Homes and apartment complexes along the coast vanished, and the First Baptist Church was leveled.

The brunt of the damage in Biloxi occurred in the east end. Along Highway 90, restaurants—including Olive Garden and Red Lobster—and St. Thomas Apostolic Catholic Church were completely washed away. The Biloxi Edgewater Village strip shopping center was demolished. Casino Row and the surrounding area south of the railroad tracks suffered almost complete devastation—the storm surge rose so high that the barges the casinos were built on drifted onto shore and into buildings. At least five casinos were put out of commission. The Gulfport Memorial Hospital in Biloxi suffered major damage.

In addition to roof damage, flooding was the most commonly reported effect of the storm in Pascagoula. The storm surge there reached 17 to 22 feet, and six blocks of Market Street were destroyed by flooding. In Moss Point, two hotels full of guests were surrounded by water. Twenty feet of water flooded most of the city, severely damaging most of the downtown area.

◇◇◇

When Paul Ruffin, on a follow-up visit to Waveland, drove up Oak Boulevard, which runs into Beach Road, he discovered Lorraine Landry walking along carrying a pot tray, which she weighted down with a rock on a propane tank and filled with water. It was a bird bath, she said. Her FEMA trailer was the only residence on the street, so she declared herself Queen of Oak Boulevard.

There are so many things that you don't really take into account when a disaster of this magnitude strikes—nowhere in all that stretch of devastation was there the sight or sound of birds. Nothing. Fewer birds than children. They were either killed outright during the hurricane or blown so far away that they decided to house somewhere inland. There was an eerie absence of birds.

Ruffin asked her when she had last seen a bird.

I saw one yesterday. We were out in a field, where they had a free breakfast and then a sermon. Right there in the middle of the sermon, I looked up and pointed and said, "Good Lord, look there! It's a bird!" I'm telling you, I was so excited, because I used to open the windows and listen and listen . . . . I mean, I used to sit out here with my binoculars, and there were birds everywhere. My cat used to sit . . . I had a porch enclosed with windows, and my cat would sit on a table, and I had a bird feeder just outside a window, and she would look at that all day long.

Alas, Queen Landry has abandoned her kingdom and retreated inland, where, it is hoped, she has found her birds.

<><><><><><><><><><><><><><><><><><><><><><><><><><><><><><><><><><><>

1445

Hurricane Katrina made its third and final landfall near Pearlington, Mississippi, and Slidell, Louisiana, with sustained winds of 120 mph after crossing Breton Sound. Authorities attribute the tremendous damage done by Katrina not to its intensity but to its size. Camille, which came ashore in virtually the same location, was much stronger but also much smaller. Katrina's storm surge is thought to have been so great because of the enormous breadth of Katrina.

Although totals are difficult to confirm because of missing persons and conflicting sources, the estimation of directly or indirectly related deaths from Katrina released by the National Hurricane Center as of 20 December 2005 was 238 in the state of Mississippi, with a total of 1,833 across five states—Louisiana, Mississippi, Florida, Georgia, and Alabama. The total for deaths directly related to Katrina's forces is 200 in Mississippi and 1,500 across four states—Louisiana, Mississippi, Florida, and Georgia. 30 of the confirmed deaths in Harrison County were in Biloxi at the St. Charles Apartment complex alone. The majority of deaths in the state were directly related to the unprecedented storm surge of over 25 feet.

Measures were taken to help those caught in the storm and prevent an even higher death toll in the state. Governor Haley Bar-

> **Destroyed Churches**
> - 14 Catholic Churches
> - 6 Episcopal Churches
> - 100 Baptist Churches (300-400 Baptist Churches Damaged)

bour mobilized units of the National Guard, calling for five battalions and six helicopters to assist with security, debris removal, and aid distribution. Some 3,000 were assembled, but they were hampered by fallen trees and other debris. Five search-and-rescue teams were sent to Biloxi and Pascagoula, and water and food distribution began on 30 August. The next day the Red Cross had 97 shelters open across the state, housing 8,500 people. Phone lines, cellular towers, and electricity were still out in Jackson and in the southern parts of the state, so the lack of communication facilities was also an obstacle to recovery efforts. General Harold A. Cross of the National Guard requested military stocks from the Pentagon's Northern Command, and FEMA medical teams arrived on 2 September, but heat in the nineties for days immediately following the hurricane further hindered the recovery effort.

According to Paul Ruffin, who interviewed several residents of the Mississippi Coast, church groups were instrumental in the relief effort. Several people commented on the helping hands of these volunteers:

Oh yeah. Believe it or not, it was the church groups that really—that the people here are most thankful for. If it hadn't of been for those church groups.... No one from FEMA or the Red Cross or anybody was seen for three weeks.

It was the church groups that came in to see that the people got food and water. We can drop food and water in these other countries on twenty-four-hour notice, but not here in our own back yard.

Church groups from all over the country came down here to help any way they could. Churches all along the Coast were destroyed,

NOAA ADVISORY 1500 UTC

...CENTER OF POWERFUL HURRICANE KATRINA AGAIN MOVING ASHORE...NEAR THE LOUISIANA-MISSISSIPPI BORDER...CONTINUES POUNDING SOUTHEASTERN LOUISIANA AND SOUTHERN MISSISSIPPI...

AT 1500 UTC THE CENTER OF HURRICANE KATRINA WAS LOCATED NEAR LAT 30.2N...LONG 89.6W. THIS POSITION IS NEAR THE MOUTH OF THE PEARL RIVER...ABOUT 35 MILES EAST-NORTHEAST OF NEW ORLEANS AND ABOUT 45 MILES WEST-SOUTHWEST OF BILOXI.

KATRINA IS MOVING TOWARD THE NORTH NEAR 16 MPH...AND THIS GENERAL MOTION IS EXPECTED TO CONTINUE TODAY AND TONIGHT. ON THIS TRACK THE CENTER WILL MOVE OVER SOUTHERN MISSISSIPPI TODAY AND INTO CENTRAL MISSISSIPPI THIS EVENING.

MAX SUSTAINED WINDS ARE NEAR 125 MPH...WITH HIGHER GUSTS.

WEAKENING IS FORECAST DURING THE NEXT 24 HOURS AS THE CENTER MOVES OVER LAND. HOWEVER...HURRICANE FORCE WINDS ARE EXPECTED TO SPREAD AS FAR AS 150 MILES INLAND ALONG THE PATH OF KATRINA.

HURRICANE FORCE WINDS EXTEND OUTWARD UP TO 125 MILES FROM THE CENTER...AND TROPICAL STORM FORCE WINDS EXTEND OUTWARD UP TO 230 MILES.

COASTAL STORM SURGE FLOODING OF 15 TO 20 FEET ABOVE NORMAL TIDE LEVELS...ALONG WITH LARGE AND DANGEROUS BATTERING WAVES...CAN BE EXPECTED NEAR AND TO THE EAST OF THE CENTER. STORM SURGE FLOODING OF 10 TO 15 FEET...NEAR THE TOPS OF THE LEVEES...IS STILL POSSIBLE IN THE GREATER NEW ORLEANS AREA.

RAINFALL TOTALS OF 5 TO 10 INCHES...WITH ISOLATED MAXIMUM AMOUNTS OF 15 INCHES...ARE POSSIBLE ALONG THE PATH OF KATRINA.

and these folks have come down to help the congregations get organized and help with tents and temporary buildings.

◇◇◇◇◇◇◇◇◇◇◇◇◇◇◇◇◇◇◇◇◇◇

Economic Impact

Katrina's impact in Mississippi reached beyond physical devastation. Thousands of jobs were lost due to severe structural damage from the storm, most significantly to casinos. Several large casinos on floating barges were damaged or destroyed when they were pushed onshore by the storm surge. Evacuees who did not, or could not, return home quickly led to a shortage of workers for the businesses that were able to reopen. Major erosion to the beaches, in addition to the destruction of other popular attractions such as casinos, led to a decrease in tourism, which many coastal towns in Mississippi rely heavily on. One Biloxi blackjack dealer estimated that the reopening of all the casinos would provide 12,000 jobs to the residents of the Mississippi coast. Even one year after Katrina hit, the revenue yields by casinos that have already reopened on three properties are still unclear. However, The Mississippi Casino Operators Association and Ascend Media Gaming reported that eight of the region's twelve casinos have reopened and estimated that gaming revenues are reaching as high as 75% of pre-storm levels.

ECONOMIC IMPACT
- $125 billion estimated amount of damage caused
- 65,380 houses in south Mississippi destroyed
- $5 billion in claims paid (as of Nov. 21)
- 141,000 Insurance claims filed in South Mississippi
- $1.3 billion in claims paid in South Mississippi
- 44 million cubic yards of debris in South Mississippi
- 21.8 million cubic yards removed (as of Dec. 5)
- $185 million spent by the Red Cross in Southern Mississippi (as of Nov. 30)

◇◇

When Paul Ruffin asked James Casey of Waveland where he managed to get groceries and household goods he replied:

Well, Wal-Mart mostly. They originally opened in a tent, somewhere around the beginning of October, and then by Thanksgiving they reopened the store itself. But if you go in

Wal-Mart, it's not like a typical Wal-Mart, more like Sam's, where everything's on pallets, and their inventory is maybe a thousandth of what it was before, but it's suiting our needs.

Many people mentioned how much help Wal-Mart had been:

Hadn't of been for Wal-Mart, we'd of starved down here.

Thank God for Wal-Mart. All the other stores just boarded up and left their stuff to rot. People broke in and got food. Can you blame them? Damned stuff was gonna rot anyhow. Can't blame the people for leaving their stores, but you can't blame the starving people for tearing down boards and taking food neither. Times was tough all the way around.

You can say what you want about Wal-Mart ruinin' this

NOAA ADVISORY 1700 UTC

...KATRINA STILL POWERFUL BUT GRADU-ALLY WEAKENING AS IT MOVES FARTHER INLAND...

AT 1700 UTC THE CENTER OF HURRICANE KATRINA WAS LOCATED NEAR LATITUDE 30.8 NORTH... LONG 89.6W OR ABOUT 40 MILES SOUTH-SOUTHWEST OF HATTIES-BURG MISSISSIPPI.

KATRINA IS MOVING TOWARD THE NORTH NEAR 17 MPH...AND THIS GENERAL MO-TION IS EXPECTED TO CONTINUE TO-DAY AND TONIGHT. ON THIS TRACK THE CENTER WILL CONTINUE MOVING OVER SOUTHERN MISSISSIPPI TODAY AND INTO CENTRAL MISSISSIPPI THIS EVENING AND TONIGHT.

MAX SUSTAINED WINDS HAVE DECREASED TO NEAR 105 MPH...

WEAKENING IS FORECAST DURING THE NEXT 24 HOURS AS THE CENTER MOVES OVER LAND. HOWEVER...HURRICANE FORCE WINDS ARE EXPECTED TO SPREAD AS FAR AS 150 MILES INLAND ALONG THE PATH OF KATRINA. SEE INLAND HURRI-CANE AND TROPICAL STORM WARNINGS FROM NATIONAL WEATHER SERVICE FORE-CAST OFFICES.

HURRICANE FORCE WINDS EXTEND OUT-WARD UP TO 125 MILES FROM THE CEN-TER...AND TROPICAL STORM FORCE WINDS EXTEND OUTWARD UP TO 230 MILES. FAR FROM THE CENTER...DAUPHIN ISLAND AL-ABAMA REPORTED SUSTAINED WINDS OF 76 MPH WITH A GUST TO 102 MPH...MOBILE ALABAMA REPORTED A WIND GUST TO 83 MPH...AND PENSACOLA FLORIDA REPORT-ED SUSTAINED WINDS OF 52 MPH WITH A GUST TO 69 MPH.

COASTAL STORM SURGE FLOODING ALONG THE NORTHERN AND NORTHEASTERN GULF OF MEXICO COAST WILL BEGIN TO SLOWLY SUBSIDE LATER TODAY.

RAINFALL TOTALS OF 5 TO 10 INCHES... WITH ISOLATED MAXIMUM AMOUNTS OF 15 INCHES...ARE POSSIBLE ALONG THE PATH OF KATRINA

country, but they saved us on the Mississippi Coast. You better believe it.

◇◇

Some hotels whose occupants during the past year were brought in by insurance companies while assessing damage are now facing high vacancies. These hotels had depended largely on tourism prior to the hurricane. With the erosion to its beaches and the slow recovery of its gambling industry, the Mississippi Coast has struggled to attract this vital contributor to its economy.

The local gaming and hotel industries suffered major economic damages from Katrina, but the effects were also felt by the nation as gas prices began to increase. The Gulf Coast is a crucial region for the country's oil industry's production, importation, and refining of petroleum. Several major Gulf Coast refineries had to shut down because of pipeline damage and power outages caused by Katrina. As of 31 August the refining capacity of up to 1.8 million barrels a day was offline. The already challenged national fuel system lost about 45 million gallons of gasoline per day. The Mississippi refineries that were offline as of 30 August included Chevron's 325,000 barrel per day refinery in Pascagoula, Ergon Refining's 23,000 barrel per day refinery in Vicksburg, and Hunt Southland's 11,000 barrel per day Sandersville refinery and 5,800 barrel per day Lumberton refinery.

◇◇

When Michael Dunican asked why Robert of Pass Christian was carrying a gun, he had this to say:

I'm carrying a gun because the looting is incredible. I had an ex-wife lived right next door, her house was washed into the middle of the street and when she returned to it everything inside had been taken, and if it wasn't something of value, then it was thrown out on the street, if they didn't want it they were going to ruin it.

I drive a Chevy Blazer, so I loaded that thing up with any valuables I had. I managed to save most of my stuff, photos, family heirlooms, photography and stereo equipment, but I lost my Mercedes and a BMW, not to mention my house, foundation and all. Funny thing is, my property is worth more now that it's houseless.

This wasn't the safest neighborhood. Your neighbors were always stealing your stuff. The most common crime was the perfect crime, stealing lawnmowers. Who's going to question a guy pushing a lawnmower?

Images from Mississippi

Only the bolted-down belfry of this church remains—services go on in the Quonset hut.

The remains of a formerly busy docking station

No one will be showering here for quite some time.

We all need angels watching over us.

James and Norma Necaise clean up and stack bricks from their leveled Waveland home.

12.16.2005 00:20

Books, journals, photo albums: some of the hardest stuff to lose

Katrina didn't bother entering the security code.

James Casey would probably agree: any pot after a storm.

Is nothing sacred to this beast?

Katrina left the lid up.

When all your worldly possessions are destroyed, your faith is all you have left.

This gentleman and his wife rode out the storm in the cinderblock safe-house behind him.

Katrina destroyed any and everything in its path.

There is nothing comfortable about this post-Katrina camp.

Triumph of the human spirit

The Hard Rock never had the chance to see the light of day.

It was ready for a grand opening, but Katrina doused the party.

All that remains is a cry for help, and an address.

At least the white picket fence and commode were spared.

12.17.2005 00:39

Lakeshore Baptist Church, Pearlington: No church, no people, but here is the steeple

Members of an Assembly of God church from Florida take a break.

A tent on the beach at Pearlington, before it a useless fire hydrant

What's left of an apartment complex in Biloxi

Biloxi fire station gets new bay window, courtesy of Hurricane Katrina.

Shaken by Camille, brought down by Katrina: the causeway leading to Biloxi from Ocean Springs.

This bumper car is a long way from the court.

One of the few surviving homes on the beach in Waveland. A man and his wife weathered the storm in the attic.

Katrina turned this church into a skate park for children.

No security door could stand up to Katrina.

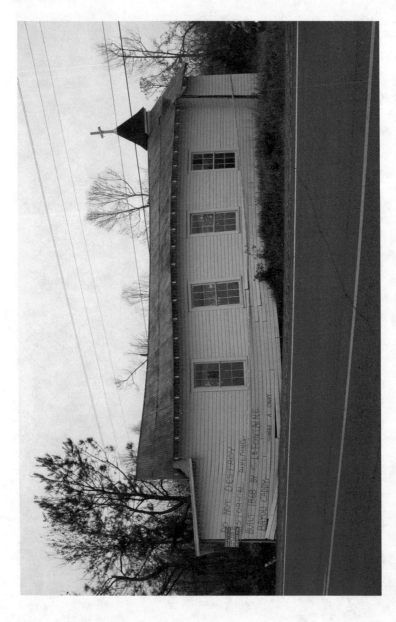

Historic church (built in 1868) in Pearlington washed across road. The entire wall is missing on opposite side.

Children in their Quonset hut classroom at St. Claire's Catholic School smile and wait for Christmas.

An empty Wal-Mart—but not for long

Old Glory was everywhere among the ruins.

All traces of civilization lost.

The largest of the live oaks were able to survive.

Remains of an insurance executive's home on South Beach Road, Waveland

Microwave hit by macrowave.

So many stairs leading nowhere.

Insurance executive's swimming pool (center background) and tennis court (right background)

Jeff Watts waits not—just weeks after the storm he has his new foundation ready.

You loot we shoot was a pervasive warning along the Coast.

Work shortage leads to temporary pay raises.

Tire swing—what a ride it would have been.

Katrina's art: an example of her metal work titled *Bad Bus*

Hey, park it wherever you can.

Luck of the roll of the dice at a homesite in Waveland

Expression of hope on steps leading to nowhere

Keeping vigil before a placid Gulf.

Nearly every homesite had a treasure trove.

We are staying, the sign says. Uh-huh, after Katrina has gone . . . .

12.16.2005 01:15

Dr. David Skagerberg dries rugs on his slab while gazing out at the Gulf.

Bedraggled bunny awaits Easter.

Entrance to Waveland Avenue from Beach Road before Katrina strikes

Entrance to Waveland Avenue from Beach Road after Katrina strikes

04·23·2006 00:07

Lorraine Landry, Queen of Oak Boulevard, waits for the birds to return. (Note makeshift bird bath at left)

Bloody but Unbowed: Katrina and Alabama

While most people are familiar with the devastation that Katrina caused in Louisiana and Mississippi, few know how much residents in Alabama were affected by the storm. Alabama did not face the full force of the eye like its western neighbors, but the path Katrina tore through the Gulf Coast was extremely wide. Most of the damage in Alabama occurred along the western coast of the state and resulted from the massive storm surge Katrina created.

Even though the eye of the storm made landfall nearly one hundred miles to the west, residents in Mobile Bay still felt its ferocity. In Alabama, the flooding and storm surge destroyed hundreds of homes and left over 624,000 residents without power. Overall, the damage was not nearly as massive as that suffered in Louisiana or Mississippi, but the citizens of communities like Bayou La Batre, Dauphin Island, and Mobile endured a severe pummeling from Katrina.

Down on the Bayou

A small fishing village of just over 2,000 citizens, Bayou La Batre claims the title of "Seafood Capital of Alabama." Despite its size, the town is a major center for seafood processing and shipbuilding in Mobile Bay. Fans of *Forrest Gump* might recognize it as Benjamin Buford "Bubba" Blue's home town. In the fiction version, Forrest makes a fortune harvesting shrimp after Hurricane Carmen destroys all his competition. Unfortunately for most citizens of Bayou La Batre, Hurricane Katrina brought no such blessings.

The ten- to fifteen-foot storm surge that swept through the community tossed shrimp boats around like bathtub toys, some of them as long as eighty feet and weighing more than one hundred tons. Over eighty boats were torn from their moorings by the surge, and around two dozen could be found in the oak and pine forests several hundred yards away from their original resting places. In addition to the loss of their livelihood, a majority of the people living in Bayou La Batre lost their homes. Roughly 1,700 people were instantly homeless after Katrina's storm surge hit their houses. With their shrimping fleet destroyed, or at least relocated, the residents of Bayou La Batre were given little hope for a positive future. And while some rebuilding efforts have started, progress has been slow.

As late as one year after Katrina rolled through the Gulf Coast, dozens of shrimping vessels were stranded in various areas around Bayou La Batre. Some were even still suspended in trees. Owners who had the funds to have their boats insured were able to recover their vessels. Those who lacked insurance, however, were still trying to come up with the money to have their boats moved or petitioning the government for assistance. The batteries and fuel were removed from the boats by the Coast Guard so they would not be a public hazard, but little else was done to get the ships back to their original locations. In the spring of 2006, the city received over $1.5 million to recover the shrimping vessels, but money was not the only barrier preventing the resolution of the issue. Many of the boats were stranded in protected wetlands or around Indian burial grounds. Since they did not want to disturb these areas, the Army Corps of Engineers was faced with an enormous logistical problem.

The boat owners were not the only people affected by Katrina's reorganization of the shrimping fleet. Each boat usually requires three workers to function properly. So for every boat out of commission, three potential jobs are unavailable. That is just the beginning of the impact for Bayou La Batre. Wholesale seafood markets that rely on the shrimping industry to run effectively have been impacted by the decreased number of working shrimp boats, and seafood is the backbone of Bayou La Batre. While some have suggested converting the area into a French styled village to focus on tourism, many residents just want to get back to the lives they had before Katrina. But most doubt that the small fishing village will ever return to its full strength and vitality.

Shifting Sands

The residents of Dauphin Island have always lived with the potential devastation hurricanes can cause. They survived large storms like Frederic and Ivan in the past, and many homeowners have experience rebuilding their houses.

Over 1,500 homes on Dauphin Island witnessed the periphery force of Katrina. Around 300 of those houses were destroyed by the storm, and many others suffered major damage. Because of the beating delivered by Hurricane Ivan the previous year, which resulted in severe erosion of the beaches, Dauphin Island residents were left with little protection.

Katrina's storm surge of over fifteen feet devastated the western end of the island and damaged or totally destroyed hundreds of homes. Since many of the roads were washed away as well, officials had difficulty inventorying the damage in some areas.

Katrina tore the offshore oil rig known as the *Ocean Warwick* from its moorings over sixty miles away and pushed it to the shore of Dauphin Island. Knowing the potential damage a powerful hurricane can cause, most residents chose to evacuate rather than to face the storm. Thus, Katrina caused no casualties on Dauphin Island.

Even a year later, many homes are in the same condition that they were just after Katrina hit. But most residents are looking to rebuild and prevent further damage in the future. For years, Dauphin Islanders have been trying to prevent erosion from eating away their beaches and destroying their protection from storms. The property owners' association worked with the city and state governments to construct a system of berms to lessen the toll that large storms like Katrina would take on the residents' homes.

Despite the berm system, the island has been slowly drifting toward the Alabama coast, and residents are losing property. Hurricane Ivan virtually eliminated the major berm in 2004, but most Dauphin Island residents feel that the US Army Corps of Engineers should bear most of the responsibility for the receding coastline.

The Army Corps has been dredging Mobile Bay for years and dumping the deposits in the deep water of the Gulf of Mexico. Many Dauphin Islanders claim that this has caused the erosion of their property. They initiated a lawsuit in 2000 against the Army Corps, charging that the dredging operation was stealing their property and thus violating their rights. In September of 2006, the court ruled in favor of an ongoing study to investigate the claims of the residents to determine whether or not the Army Corps should be held responsible for the migration of the island.

Not all homeowners on Dauphin Island have been idle while waiting for a resolution to the issue of losing property. Most of the homes that were destroyed or damaged still remain as Katrina left them over a year ago, but renovation is underway in many areas. Despite their determination to rebuild, residents of Dauphin Island still face many challenges.

Repairing and rebuilding the island's infrastructure presents one of the largest problems for the city and home owners. FEMA spent over $750 million replacing water pumps and lines. But problems still remain. Some of the infrastructure, such as pipes and manholes on the west end, will be underwater for extended periods because of the land lost to erosion.

Large portions of Bienville Boulevard, the island's main thoroughfare, still have not yet been paved. The force of Katrina's waves ripped up sections of the road and washed them away. Other areas were left with high and low undulations, mirroring the waves that washed over them. Some of the road has been temporarily repaired, but city and state officials are developing a more thorough reconstruction project.

Much of the restoration involves establishing a new system to prevent further land loss of the island. Beach erosion has left many areas vulnerable to high tides, and heavy rainstorms can cause flooding on the western end of the island. In order to secure federal funds to continue restoration, some members of the property owners' association have suggested turning three and a half miles of the western part of the island over to the town of Dauphin Island. Many residents disagree with this action, however, and suggest that valuable property should not be exchanged for short-term relief.

Returning to a normal life still seems like a distant goal to many residents of Dauphin Island, but they are working toward that end. Despite millions of dollars in damage and the destruction of hundreds of homes, most feel fortunate to have survived the storm with a chance to rebuild. Reconstruction may move at a slower pace than desired, but residents are glad to see some progress.

The Royalty of the Bay

Over 200,000 residents of Mobile were affected by Hurricane Katrina. An eight- to ten-foot storm surge, combined with torrential rainfall, caused massive flooding throughout the city. Although Hurricane Ivan caused more damage in 2004, many homes and businesses were still devastated by Katrina.

Floodwaters that reached as high as eleven feet flowed through the city as Katrina moved eastward. Mobile had not seen flooding on that level for nearly ninety years. In parts of the city only the tops of parking meters were visible, and buildings in downtown Mobile became manmade islands in a sea created by the rain and storm surge.

Nearly 400,000 homes in Mobile and surrounding communities were damaged by the waters, and many businesses suffered as well. Floodwaters damaged buildings and inventories and kept many potential customers away.

The waters were powerful enough to tear an oil rig from its moorings in a repair yard on the bay. Katrina pushed the rig into the bay and into the Mobile River, where it was eventually stopped by the Cochrane/Africatown USA bridge. The bridge, known as a landmark and symbol of modernity in Alabama, was struck hard by the oil platform but did not receive substantial damage.

Many residents lost their homes, while others faced significant damage. Although they are trying to return to normalcy, they are often hampered by insurance and government paperwork. As in many other areas affected by Katrina, reconstruction in Mobile has moved at a slower pace than most would prefer.

The Heart of Dixie Continues Beating

FEMA has spent over $5 million in disaster aid in Alabama—nearly 3,000 households received direct aid from the federal government. Over 1,500 travel trailers and mobile homes were provided to Alabama residents who lost their homes. Almost one thousand households are still living in FEMA trailers. A year after Katrina destroyed their homes, most of these families were given the option to either buy the FEMA trailers or find other housing.

When viewed mathematically, the amount of damage in Alabama pales in comparison to Louisiana and Mississippi. But those affected are not looking at the numbers. Many residents in Alabama feel like they were neglected by the rest of the country. With all the attention given to the devastation in other areas, Alabama has received little coverage. While residents of places like New Orleans and Biloxi are concerned that the rest of the country has forgotten their struggles a year after Katrina ripped through their lives, those in Bayou La Batre, Dauphin Island, and Mobile have a different complaint. As one resident claims, "We weren't forgotten. We were never recognized."

Images of Katrina and Alabama

A satellite image of Dauphin Island showing the oil rig *Ocean Warwick*, now sixty miles away from its original location

Many houses on Dauphin Island were damaged by Katrina's storm surge.

One major difficulty in reconstruction was moving all the sand washed up by Katrina.

Katrina relocated the walkway to this dock.

Once a home, only the stilts remain after Katrina blew through.

A mattress—half-submerged by the sands Katrina washed onto Dauphin Island

Who knows where the house is that this ceiling fan belonged to?

More household items relocated by the storm

Damage from Katrina's storm surge on Dauphin Island

This house was quickly abandoned before Katrina hit.

The blender remained on the counter, margarita mix still inside.

A reflection of a desolate home

Many houses still remain in disrepair a year after the storm.

Shrimp boats that Katrina tossed about like toys lie beached and abandoned.

The Beast That Would Not Die:
Katrina Tracks to the North

On Monday, 29 August, at approximately 1800, Hurricane Katrina's center of circulation pushed ashore along the central Gulf Coast, quickly weakening to Category 1. Just six hours later, northwest of Meridian, Mississippi, Katrina was reclassified as a tropical storm, rainfall becoming the primary threat, with amounts exceeding two to four inches from the Gulf Coast to the Ohio River Valley. As a result, flood watches and warnings were posted all across these regions, leading to widespread evacuations. But Katrina's devastation continued in outer rain bands that spiraled into other areas of the country, spawning tornadoes that caused considerable damage.

Georgia was hit hardest with more than three inches of rain and tornadoes—with ratings of F0, F1, and F2 on the Fujita Scale—that damaged homes, poultry houses, and businesses, and knocked down thousands of trees in the northern and central parts of the state. Several people were injured, and there was at least one fatality.

The most serious of the tornadoes was the first of the day. It struck portions of Heard and Carroll counties west of Atlanta around 1625, causing at least three injuries and one fatality as several homes were severely damaged, large poultry barns completely destroyed, and over 140,000 chicks killed. This was an F2 tornado. Two more F2 tornadoes occurred later in the evening, one in Peach County south of Macon, and the other in White County northeast of Gainesville. Injuries were reported in the Peach County storm, as well as in another tornado in Spalding County south of Atlanta. Other counties hit by tornadoes (rated F0 or F1) included Walton, Barrow, Hall, Polk, Haralson, Fannin, Lumpkin, Paulding, Oconee, Jackson, Forsyth, and Taylor in northern and central Georgia, and in Decatur County and Evans County in South Georgia. By the end of the day there had been at least eighteen tornadoes, the most on record in that state for one day in August.

Katrina was finally downgraded to a tropical depression near Clarksville, Tennessee, where the storm broke in half, sending one half racing northward, affecting the central United States along its path, while the other headed for the eastern part of the Appalachians, extending the already significant tornado outbreak in the area of Alabama and central Georgia up to central Pennsylvania.

These outbreaks killed two people, injured several, and caused millions of dollars in additional damage. Katrina continued to weaken as it moved inland, but tropical-storm-force gusts were recorded as far north as Fort Campbell, Kentucky, on 30 August. A storm that had moved through the weekend before had already produced flooding, and the rainfall from Katrina added more rains to the saturated soil. As a result, Kentucky's Governor, Ernie Fletcher, declared three counties disaster areas and declared a state of emergency for all of Kentucky. One person was killed in Hopkinsville, Kentucky, and part of a high school collapsed. Flooding also prompted a number of evacuations in West Virginia, and in Ohio the rainfall led to two indirect deaths. Katrina caused a number of power outages in many areas, with over 100,000 customers affected in Tennessee, primarily in the Memphis and Nashville areas. The remnants of the storm brought high levels of rainfall to a wide swath of the eastern United States, and rain in excess of two inches fell in parts of twenty states. A number of tornadoes associated with Katrina formed on 30 and 31 August, causing minor damages in several regions. A total of 62 tornadoes formed in eight states as a result of Katrina.

Meanwhile, the remnants of the northbound half of Katrina were last distinguishable in the eastern Great Lakes region on 31 August before being absorbed by a frontal boundary and becoming a powerful extratropical low pressure system, causing rainfall of two to six inches in twelve hours, as well as gale-force wind gusts from 31 to 61 mph in southeastern Quebec and northern New Brunswick. In the region of Saguenay and Cote-Nord, rain caused breakdowns and failure in roads. The Cote-Nord region was isolated from rest of Quebec for at least a week.

New York

Western New York had many reports of flooding, as well as damage caused by fallen trees from Katrina's wind and rain. At least

4,500 customers were left without power in the Buffalo and Rochester areas.

Damage from wind and flooding was also reported in the northern part of the state, near the Ontario border. About 1,100 customers lost power in that area.

Ohio

In Ohio, some flooding and power outages were reported, including about 2,500 in the easternmost part of the state alone, and several areas were evacuated throughout the state. One hospital in Dennison had to be evacuated when it lost power and its generator failed. Two deaths were blamed on the storm in Ohio, both indirect deaths from an accident caused by Katrina's rains in the Monroeville area.

A tornado hit Warren County on 30 August, causing minor damage in Morrow and Salem Township. Three houses were damaged, but no injuries were reported.

Ontario

On 30 August heavy rain and tropical-storm-force wind gusts were reported in Southern Ontario as Katrina passed over the area before dissipating into a remnant low in the east. Port Colborne and Brockville appeared to receive the most rain, both with over four inches. Other regions in the province reported one to two inches, except near the New York border, where up to three inches was reported. There were also some scattered reports of flooding and damage due to fallen trees.

Pennsylvania

In Pennsylvania, at least two tornadoes spawned from Katrina's outer bands and touched down in south-central part of the state south of Harrisburg. Numerous trees were brought down, and several roofs were damaged.

Quebec

On 31 August the storm system previously known as Katrina was partially absorbed by a front and continued to produce heavy rainfall down the St. Lawrence River Valley. Several villages in the northeastern part of Quebec were isolated due to multiple washouts. Sections of roads were destroyed, effectively cutting these villages off from land travel. Affected areas were supplied by boats normally supplying the Magdalen Islands. The system crossed over uninhabited areas of Labrador before completely dissipating.

Tennessee

At the storm's peak, at least 80,000 customers were without power, primarily in the Memphis and Nashville areas. Most damage was caused by fallen trees. However, there were no deaths or injuries reported in Tennessee as a result of Katrina.

Virginia

In Virginia, a tornado related to Katrina's outer bands touched down in Marshall, damaging at least thirteen homes. In addition, around 4,000 customers lost electricity. No deaths or injuries were reported.

West Virginia

Significant flooding was reported in several communities in West Virginia, including Sissonville, forcing some local evacuations.

The Most Helpless Victims: Katrina and the Animals

One forgotten group of victims of Hurricane Katrina is the myriad pets, wildlife, farm animals, and marine life that suffered from displacement, abandonment, starvation, dehydration, and death. The plight of animals was first brought compellingly to the nation's attention in a news report on the evacuation of Superdome inhabitants to Houston, Texas, in which a young boy getting on a bus was forced to give up his little white dog, Snowball. A police officer took the dog, and the boy cried so hard that he made himself sick. Sympathetic watchers created a fund to offer a $3,000 reward to whoever could reunite the boy with his dog, and websites sprang up to help find lost pets.

Several people refused to leave their pets behind, choosing to face perilous conditions in order to ensure the safety of their animals. These owners were distressed because they felt that their animals were helpless and depended on them for safety—leaving them behind seemed cruel. Similarly, one dog refused to leave the side of its owner, even after the man had died and been covered with a blanket. The dog stayed there for days. Many pets were left in their homes with food and water by owners who expected to return in a few days to retrieve them. Other owners tried to take their pets with them when they evacuated, only to be forced to leave them behind. Officers and rescuers who did not allow animals on rescue boats and evacuation buses did so in the interest of saving human lives.

Some pets were left alone to survive in the severe weather conditions or were trapped in cages, and some that made it through the storm died later from starvation or dehydration. Dogs swam until they were rescued or found higher ground or drowned. In the Superdome, some animals were kept in a stairwell, where they would be protected from the elements.

Although the attention of the media was not immediately focused on animals following Katrina's impact, the Humane Society of the United States' (HSUS) National Disaster Animal Response Team (DART) began preparing for a large response as soon as they received word of the hurricane's path. Prior to the impact, the Louisiana Society for the Prevention of Cruelty to Animals (SPCA) evacuated its animals in accordance with the facility's disaster response plan, so the shelter was able to house animals rescued in the aftermath of Katrina. Over thirty HSUS rescue staff members and volunteers from twelve states came together with state officials, federal agencies, and other rescue organizations to search for animals. They set up shelters, distributed supplies, and provided medical help. The HSUS animal response units were stationed near some of the worst-hit regions in Mississippi and Louisiana, but some disaster teams heading into New Orleans had to wait in Baton Rouge until Governor Blanco lifted evacuation orders. Other teams were hindered by severe flooding, which limited access and posed severe health threats to rescuers. The flood water contained oil, sewage, gas, and chemicals, and animals retrieved from these conditions could be treated only by workers who had been vaccinated for Hepatitis A and B because of the exposure to human waste. DART was prepared to help family pets as well as large animals, keeping a stock of cages, leads, harnesses, and slings used for lifting.

Facilities housing marine and exotic animals, like zoos, aquariums, and animal parks, could not be evacuated, so the animals and their caretakers had to ride out the storm. Transporting so many animals would have required more preparation time, but even with plenty of warning, the process would have been too dangerous for most large and exotic animals, and there were few places for any of them to go. The Marine Life Oceanarium in Gulfport, Mississippi, which was completely destroyed by the storm, evacuated six dolphins to hotel swimming pools before sending them to facilities in Florida. Nine sea lions from the Oceanarium were sent to Florida as well. The New Orleans' Audubon Aquarium, a facility that houses 10,000 animals, lost only a few flamingoes.

Dangerous wildlife displaced by the storm, such as alligators and poisonous snakes, posed safety threats to people and other animals. Even relatively harmless wild animals acted out of defense and became aggressive when humans attempted to release them from debris, transport them out of dangerous areas, or treat their injuries. Volunteers were encouraged not to deal with these animals, placing them lower on the list of priorities in the rescue effort.

Farms in Alabama, Georgia, Mississippi, Florida, and

Louisiana, all of which suffered damage from Hurricane Katrina, significantly contribute to the United States' meat, egg, and dairy industries each year. Power losses, forceful winds, flooding, and hot temperatures yielded perilous conditions for poultry, cattle, and pigs. Floods of saltwater and depleted food sources were major threats to thousands of cattle in Louisiana. Operations at many animal factories were disrupted by structural damage and power outages. Facilities using automated watering, feeding, and ventilation systems lost all these functions when the power went out, leaving animals to face severe temperatures without food or water. One chicken broiler farm in Mississippi, the nation's fourth largest poultry producing state, lost all but roughly one thousand chickens, which were rescued from among decomposing chicken corpses by an HSUS response team.

Though there is no way of knowing an exact figure, the scope of animal deaths was staggering despite the efforts of so many animal rescue staff members and volunteers. Animals faced many dangers, and not all people handled them with care. In Saint Bernard Parish, Louisiana, when the levees broke, hundreds of people fled to schools. They took their pets with them, and a few even picked up strays on the way. They sought refuge from the floodwaters in Sebastian Roy Elementary School, Beauregard Middle School, and Saint Bernard High School. After a few days, police officers forced everyone to board trucks, which began their evacuation to other parts of the United States, assuring them that they would take all the animals to a shelter for safety. Two to four weeks after leaving the schools, the refugees returned to be re-united with their pets, only to find most of the dogs and cats dead in the rooms where they had been left. Most of them had been shot. These devastated pet owners, who had entrusted their animals to the officers, claimed that it was the officers themselves who had shot the animals after police-issued ammunition and shells were discovered at the schools. The case is still under investigation, and motives behind the shootings are still unknown. Although a few of the animals escaped and one dog had been overlooked where it was stuck behind a filing cabinet, over thirty animals were shot.

In the same county, Pulitzer Prize winning photographer David Leeson, Jr. filmed police officers shooting stray and abandoned animals in the street around 7 September. He was there filming the devastation of the storm in the days immediately following Katrina and paused to help a dog, which he says was shot right in front of him. The audio of his tape captures the sounds of eight or nine dogs being shot, and in Leeson's on-camera interview with one of the policemen, the officer admitted that he had been killing dogs. Leeson's footage has been turned over to the attorney general's office.

Images of Katrina's Animal Victims

A stray in the Lower Ninth Ward seeks drier ground.

A few of the many animals that were rescued

A concerned rescue worker feeds a helpless puppy after the storm.

This tiny kitten would never have survived without the help of volunteers.

Two frightened pets saved by rescuers

This dolphin was transported to a hotel pool.

Many animals required special care after being rescued.

Two dogs, waiting for a ride

Messages were left to let owners know that their pets were dead.

Strays were often forced to beg for food from strangers.

He made it halfway through the gate.

So many were not saved, despite all the heroic efforts.

Appendix

The Saffir-Simpson Hurricane Scale*

The Saffir-Simpson Hurricane Scale is a 1-5 rating based on a hurricane's intensity. This is used to project an estimate of the potential property damage and flooding expected along the coast from a hurricane landfall. Wind speed is the determining factor in the scale, as storm-surge values are highly dependent on the slope of the continental shelf and the shape of the coastline in the landfall region. It should be noted that all winds are using the US one-minute average.

Category 1 Hurricane:

Winds 74-95 mph (64-82 kt or 119-153 km/hr). Storm surge generally four to five feet above normal. No real damage to building structures. Damage primarily to unanchored mobile homes, shrubbery, and trees. Some damage to poorly constructed signs. Also, some coastal road flooding and minor pier damage. Hurricane Lili (2002) made landfall on the Louisiana coast as a Category 1 hurricane. Hurricane Gaston (2004) was a Category 1 hurricane that made landfall along the central South Carolina coast.

Category 2 Hurricane:

Winds 96-110 mph (83-95 kt or 154-177 km/hr). Storm surge generally six to eight feet above normal. Some roofing material, door, and window damage to buildings. Considerable damage to shrubbery and trees with some trees blown down. Considerable damage to mobile homes, poorly constructed signs, and piers. Coastal and low-lying escape routes flood two to four hours before arrival of the hurricane center. Small craft

*Provided by the NOAA website.

in unprotected anchorages break moorings. Hurricane Frances (2004) made landfall over the southern end of Hutchinson Island, Florida, as a Category 2 hurricane. Hurricane Isabel (2003) made landfall near Drum Inlet on the Outer Banks of North Carolina as a Category 2 hurricane.

Category 3 Hurricane:

Winds 111-130 mph (96-113 kt or 178-209 km/hr). Storm surge generally nine to twelve feet above normal. Some structural damage to small residences and utility buildings with a minor amount of curtainwall failures. Damage to shrubbery and trees, with foliage blown off and large trees blown down. Destruction of mobile homes and poorly constructed signs. Rising water cuts low-lying escape routes three to five hours before arrival of the center of the hurricane. Flooding near the coast destroys smaller structures, with larger structures damaged by battering from floating debris. Terrain continuously lower than five feet above mean sea level may be flooded inland eight miles or more. Evacuation of low-lying residences within several blocks of the shoreline may be required. Hurricanes Jeanne and Ivan (2004) were Category 3 hurricanes when they made landfall in Florida and Alabama, respectively.

Category 4 Hurricane:

Winds 131-155 mph (114-135 kt or 210-249 km/hr). Storm surge generally thirteen to eighteen feet above normal. More extensive curtainwall failures with some complete roof structure failures on small residences. Wind blows down shrubs, trees, and all signs. Complete destruction of mobile homes. Extensive damage to doors and windows. Rising water may cut low-lying escape routes three to five hours before arrival of the center of the hurricane. Major damage to lower floors of structures near the shore. Terrain lower than ten feet above sea level may be flooded, requiring massive evacuation of residential areas as far as six miles inland. Hurricane Charley (2004) was a Category 4 hurricane that made landfall in Charlotte County, Florida, with winds of 150 mph. Hurricane Dennis (2005) struck the island of Cuba as a Category 4 hurricane.

Category 5 Hurricane:

Winds greater than 155 mph (135 kt or 249 km/hr). Storm surge generally greater than eighteen feet above normal. Complete roof failure on many residences and industrial buildings. Some complete building failures with small utility buildings blown over or away. Most shrubs, trees, and signs blown down. Complete destruction of mobile homes. Severe and extensive window and door damage. Low-lying escape routes are cut by rising water three to five hours before arrival of the center of the hurricane. Major damage to lower floors of all structures located lower than fifteen feet above sea level and within 500 yards of the shoreline. Massive evacuation of residential areas on low ground within five to ten miles of the shoreline may be required. Only three Category 5 hurricanes have made landfall in the United States since records began: The Labor Day Hurricane of 1935, Hurricane Camille (1969), and Hurricane Andrew (1992). The 1935 Labor Day Hurricane struck the Florida Keys with a minimum pressure of 892 mb—the lowest pressure ever observed in the United States. Hurricane Camille struck the Mississippi Gulf Coast, causing a 25-foot storm surge, which inundated Pass Christian. Hurricane Andrew of 1992 made landfall over southern Miami-Dade County, Florida, causing 26.5 billion dollars in losses—at that time the costliest hurricane on record. In addition, Hurricane Wilma (2005) was a Category Five hurricane at peak intensity and is the strongest Atlantic tropical cyclone on record, with a minimum pressure of 882 mb.

Mississippi Counties Directly Affected by Hurricane Katrina

1)   Jefferson

2)   Adams

3)   Franklin

4)   Lincoln

5)   Lawrence

6)   Jefferson Davis

7)   Covington

8)   Jones

9)   Wayne

10)   Wilkinson

11)   Amite

12)   Pike

13)   Walthall

14)   Marion

15)   Lamar

16)   Forrest

17)   Perry

18)   Greene

19)   Pearl River

20)   Stone

21)   George

22)   Hancock

23)   Harrison

24)   Jackson

GLOSSARY

Depression
A region of low atmospheric pressure that is usually accompanied by low clouds and precipitation. The term is also sometimes used as a reference to a Tropical Depression.

Eye
The relatively calm center in a hurricane that is more than one half surrounded by wall cloud. The winds are light, the skies are partly cloudy or even clear (the skies are usually free of rain), and radar depicts it as an echo-free area within the eye wall.

Eye Wall
An organized band of cumuliform clouds that immediately surrounds the center (eye) of a hurricane. The fiercest winds and most intense rainfall typically occur near the eye wall. Eye wall and wall cloud are used synonymously, but it should not be confused with a wall cloud of a thunderstorm.

Hurricane
A tropical cyclone with surface winds in excess of 74 mph (64 knots) in the Western Hemisphere. There are various regional names for these storms.

Hurricane Season
The portion of the year having a relatively high incidence of hurricanes. The hurricane season in the Atlantic, Caribbean, and Gulf of Mexico runs from 1 June to 30 November. The hurricane season in the Eastern Pacific basin runs from 15 May to 30 November. The hurricane season in the Central Pacific basin runs from 1 June to 30 November.

Hurricane Warning
A warning that sustained winds 74 mph (64 kt) or higher associated with a hurricane are expected in a specified coastal area in 24 hours or less. A hurricane warning can remain in effect when dangerously high water or a combination of dangerously high water and exceptionally

high waves continue, even though winds may be less than hurricane force.

Hurricane Watch
An announcement of specific coastal areas that a hurricane or an incipient hurricane condition poses a possible threat, generally within 36 hours

Millibar (mb)
A unit of atmospheric pressure equal to 1/1000 bar, or 1000 dynes per square centimeter.

Ridge
An elongated area of relatively high atmospheric pressure—the opposite of trough.

Shear
Variation in wind speed (speed shear) and/or direction (directional shear) over a short distance within the atmosphere. Shear usually refers to vertical wind shear, i.e., the change in wind with height, but the term also is used in Doppler radar to describe changes in radial velocity over short horizontal distances.

Storm Surge
A rise above the normal water level along a shore caused by strong onshore winds and/or reduced atmospheric pressure. The surge height is the difference between the observed water level and the predicted tide. Most hurricane deaths are caused by the storm surge. It can be fifty or more miles wide and sweeps across the coastline near the point where the hurricane makes landfall. The maximum rises in sea-level move from under the storm to the right of the storm's track, reaching a maximum amplitude of up to thirty feet at the coast. The storm surge may even double in height when the hurricane's track causes it to funnel water into a bay. The storm surge increases substantially as it approaches the land because the normal water depth decreases rapidly as it approaches the beaches. The moving water contains the same amount of energy, thus resulting in an increase of storm surge. Typically, the stronger the hurricane, the greater the storm surge.

Tropical Cyclone

A warm-core, non-frontal, synoptic-scale cyclone, originating over tropical or subtropical waters, with organized deep convection and a closed surface wind circulation about a well-defined center. Once formed, a tropical cyclone is maintained by the extraction of heat energy from the ocean at high temperatures and heat export at the low temperatures of the upper troposphere. In this they differ from extratropical cyclones, which derive their energy from horizontal temperature contrasts in the atmosphere (baroclinic effects).

Tropical Depression

Cyclones that have maximum sustained winds or surface wind speed of 38 mph (32 kph) or less. They are located in either the tropics or subtropics. They characteristically have one or more closed isobars. They usually intensify slowly and may dissipate before reaching Tropical Storm intensity.

Tropical Wave

A trough or cyclonic curvature maximum in the trade wind easterlies and not classified as a tropical cyclone. The wave may reach maximum amplitude in the lower-middle troposphere.

Troposphere

The layer of the atmosphere from the earth's surface up to the tropopause, characterized by decreasing temperature with height, vertical wind motion, appreciable water vapor content, and sensible weather (clouds, rain, etc.).

Trough

An elongated area of relatively low atmospheric pressure, usually not associated with a closed circulation, and thus used to distinguish from a closed low. The opposite of ridge.

Typhoon

A hurricane that forms in the Western Pacific Ocean

Wind Gust

Rapid fluctuations in the wind speed with a variation of 10 knots or more between peaks and lulls. The speed of the gust will be the maximum instantaneous wind speed.

Wind Shear

The rate at which wind velocity changes from point to point in a given direction. The shear can be speed shear (where speed changes between the two points, but not direction), direction shear (where direction changes between the two points, but not speed) or a combination of the two.

The Editors

Heather Andrews earned a bachelor's degree from Dallas Baptist University and graduated with an Master of Education degree from SHSU in December of 2006. She currently teaches at the high school level.

Tameika Ashford, currently living in Houston, graduated Summa Cum Laude from Dillard University in New Orleans.

Joshua Bowen, after earning his BA and MA in History from SHSU, is pursuing his MA in English at SHSU and plans to begin a Ph.D program in American Studies.

Brandon Cooper, who earned his BA in English at East Texas Baptist University, holds an MA in Theological Studies with a Biblical Languages emphasis from Houston Baptist University. He has also done post-graduate work in Modern Hebrew at Cambridge University in Britain. After receiving his MA in English at SHSU, he plans to pursue a Ph.D. in Religion and Literature

Lesley Cort received her BA degree in English from SHSU and graduated in December of 2006 with a Master of Education in Curriculum and Instruction. She plans to seek a Ph.D. in English.

Michael Dunican earned a Bachelor of Arts in Film from Emerson College. In June of 2006 he visited Alabama, Mississippi, and Louisiana, collecting pictures and personal testimonials of Hurricane Katrina's destruction for this book. His future plans include teaching and writing.

Steven Rydarowski is pursuing an MA in English at SHSU. He spends his time playing hockey.

Melanie Sweeney is pursuing an MA (Creative Writing) at SHSU. She graduated from Texas A&M University with a BA in Speech Communication in May of 2006. Her plans for the future include writing, pursuing a Ph.D. in English, and ultimately teaching at a university.